PRECIOUS MOMENTS
IN HELL

PRECIOUS MOMENTS IN HELL

Charli

ELM HILL

A Division of
HarperCollins Christian Publishing

www.elmhillbooks.com

Precious Moments in Hell

Published in Nashville, Tennessee, by Elm Hill, an imprint of Thomas Nelson. Elm Hill and Thomas Nelson are registered trademarks of HarperCollins Christian Publishing, Inc.

Cover design by Dean Robbins.

Elm Hill titles may be purchased in bulk for educational, business, fund-raising, or sales promotional use. For information, please e-mail SpecialMarkets@ ThomasNelson.com.

Scripture quotations marked ESV are from the ESV˚ Bible (The Holy Bible, English Standard Version˚). Copyright © 2001 by Crossway, a publishing ministry of Good News Publishers. Used by permission. All rights reserved.

Scripture quotations marked GW are from God's Word˚. Copyright © 1995 God's Word to the Nations. Used by permission of Baker Publishing Group. All rights reserved.

Scripture quotations marked KJV are from the King James Version. Public domain.

Scripture quotations marked NASB are from New American Standard Bible˚. Copyright © 1960, 1962, 1963, 1968, 1971, 1972, 1973, 1975, 1977, 1995 by The Lockman Foundation. Used by permission. (www.Lockman.org)

Scripture quotations marked NIV are from the Holy Bible, New International Version˚, NIV˚. Copyright © 1973, 1978, 1984, 2011 by Biblica, Inc.˚ Used by permission of Zondervan. All rights reserved worldwide. www.Zondervan.com. The "NIV" and "New International Version" are trademarks registered in the United States Patent and Trademark Office by Biblica, Inc.˚

Scripture quotations marked NKJV are from the New King James Version˚. © 1982 by Thomas Nelson. Used by permission. All rights reserved.

Scripture quotations marked NLV are from the New Life Version. © Christian Literature International.

Scripture quotations marked NLT are from the Holy Bible, New Living Translation. © 1996, 2004, 2007, 2013, 2015 by Tyndale House Foundation. Used by permission of Tyndale House Publishers, Inc., Carol Stream, Illinois 60188. All rights reserved.

Library of Congress Cataloging-in-Publication Data

Library of Congress Control Number: 2019915894

ISBN 978-1-400328000 (Paperback)
ISBN 978-1-400328017 (Hardbound)
ISBN 978-1-400328024 (eBook)

CONTENTS

INTRODUCTION

Father, in Jesus' Name, show us Your purpose!

"And we know that for those who love God all things work together for good, for those who are called according to his purpose."

ROMANS 8:28 ESV

Albert Einstein once said, "There are only two ways to live your life. One is as though nothing is a miracle. The other is as though everything is a miracle." I know for a fact that my Savior has performed miracle after miracle in my life. I once read that, "Everyone wants a miracle. But here's the catch: no one wants to be in a situation that necessitates one!" Mark Batterson "The Grave Robber".

You might think the title *Precious Moments in Hell* is unusual. For years family and friends told me I should write a book. Yet, unless Jesus prompts me, it's in vain. After many years I finally asked, "Lord if you want me to write a book, tell me, please. Amen." The following morning I heard the words "Precious Moments in Hell." When I heard those words, I knew I had a title for all my life stories.

Precious Moments in Hell is not a title condoned by pastors or Christian folk because there is truth in what they say, "There are no precious moments in hell and damnation." Like my son says today, "True that." However, in my life here on earth I have experienced moments and years of what many people refer to as hell on earth, yet here I am with **precious moments** to tell.

What is this story?

It is God's story in my life, beginning with my childhood. It's about some of my valleys of hell on earth and the **precious moments** that God provided even in those valleys which prepared me for such a time as this.

By the time I was three I had two little brothers. The three of us survived an alcoholic mother who was a prostitute, a father who threw us away, and an abusive foster care environment where we were beaten daily. I also survived a mother murdered, a daughter abducted, and a stint as a homeless person because of a heroin addict who emptied out my bank account. God was with me through it all. God walked me through those many emotionally traumatic events in my life and I can honestly say that He is the Great Healer!

At an early age, I knew I was different. When we were just two, three, and four, my brothers and I were locked in a closet for days on end—God met us there. He did not forsake us. He had a plan and a purpose.

When I was seven, an angel dressed as a nun spoke words that I would cling to for the rest of my life. That angel told me who my Father is—what a life-saving bit of knowledge for a foster child to know she has been adopted by a King!

God gifted me with **visions** and **dreams** and has led me on amazing adventures, showing off like only God can do. He even wrote a Bible verse in the clouds. Another **vision** led me to the graphic artist who years later would design an initial cover for my book *Precious Moments in Hell*. The vision was a warning about some kind of shooting and it literally saved his life. Multiple times the dreams or visions God would give me intertwined my life with someone who God then later used for his purposes. Only God is able to coordinate the details in advance! Just like He arranged for Jesus, the Bread of Life, to be born in a town with the name of Bethlehem, which means House of Bread. He knows the beginning from the end and He works all things for good for those who are called according to his purpose.

God has moved me into various professions: truck driver, correctional officer, hospital security officer, arc welder, realtor, pastor, and others. In each season, He always had a purpose. Time and again He would lead me into the life of someone in need of prayer for a miracle. And God was faithful—He provided those miracles! One of many miracles in my life was the miraculous provisions to learn about Jesus even at the hands of an abusive foster care mom, and then the more miraculous work of taking my raging hatred—at one point I intended to kill this foster care mom—and changing it to actual love for this same woman. God can and does change hearts—that is a miracle indeed!

My purpose in sharing these stories of my valleys of hell on earth and the **precious moments** God supplied is to bring glory to my Savior and to assure you that there is hope even when you find yourself in a pit of despair. He can take your darkest days, shed light on them, and then turn your experiences for a good purpose. An example in my life was when God had directed me to a specific profession but I stubbornly resisted. He allowed me to be unemployed for 18 months by closing all doors. Believe me, being unemployed was not fun and it definitely felt like a valley. I remained in that valley until I was obedient. Once I accepted the direction he intended, He used it to bless my brother and me beyond measure—a super high mountaintop experience! Truck driving was instrumental in providing a dying man's final wish! That was one of the preplanned purposes for me needing that specific job.

I wouldn't have these amazing stories except that God, through His miraculous power, saved me from each situation which seemed like hell at the time. He rescued me time and again, pulled me out of the pits, and in each circumstance He left me with a **precious moment**.

"You, however, have followed my teaching, my conduct, my aim in life, my faith, my patience, my love, my steadfastness, my persecutions and sufferings that happened to me at Antioch, at

Iconium, and at Lystra—which persecutions I endured; yet from them all the Lord rescued me."

(2 Timothy 3:10–11 ESV)

Come with me as we walk through some of my valleys of the shadow of death as I share my trials and triumphs and **precious moments**. By the grace of God I survived my valleys and so can you!

Yes, Father in Jesus' name, the Name above all names, I plead your sacrificial Blood upon all people who are hoping for a touch from your Holy Spirit, that you will help our unbelief and fill us with more grace, more mercy. May Your will be accomplished through those who will read these pages and call out to you, especially knowing YOU are our precious moments here on Earth and forever more, amen!

SHADOW OF DEATH

*"Yea, though I walk through the valley of the shadow of death,
I will fear no evil: for thou art with **me**. "*

PSALM 23:4 KJV

There are valleys we each will walk through in this life. Psalm 23 calls them "Valleys of the Shadow of death." Some refer to them as hell on earth. God has promised to be with us always. So in each valley that we allow God to guide us through, if we open our eyes to the miracles of God we will also experience **precious moments**.

These are the true stories of a girl beginning at age four and her journey through the valleys of the shadow of death. The only true and faithful partner and friend she ever had was a Shepherd she learned about in the Bible. That Shepherd orchestrated a whisper from an angel dressed as a nun which turned out to be the very thing this little girl needed to cling to as she navigated the valleys of life. This little girl was me and although there were many hellish moments, there have been many precious moments along this tumultuous journey. This is my story—**precious moments in hell**.

Have you experienced any of these: parents who threw you away; being locked in a dark closet; foster parents who were never trained, therefore beat and/or tortured you; abused by a spouse; beaten nearly to death? Have you never been picked to be a captain, cheerleader, pitcher, catcher, or to play the infield? Have you had the love of your life leave you? Have you witnessed a murder? Has someone you love been abducted? Have you heard a cry for help and been helpless to do anything? These are just a few of the pits, caves and crevices that I have experienced in the valleys of my life. My life has been filled with many valleys—some refer to as hell on earth, but God always weaves a **precious moment** in there somewhere.

My valleys started early in life. In the beginning of my life, I shared my valley with my two younger brothers. This little girl spent the first six years of her life caring for her two little brothers. Lupe was fifteen when her daughter "Charli" was born and within the next two years, Charli had two little brothers. I am Charli.

I was four years old when I first really became aware of my life and could understand some of what was going on around me. The first memory I have is waking to the sound of my mother's scream. She was yelling for me to wake up and to get my brother, Chief, up. We ran to the wooden screen door where my mother stood holding my baby brother Little Leroy in her arms. The barn was on fire! Our father had opened the barn doors so the animals could escape. In the chaos, it was as if my eyes were opened for the first time and I realized I was alive. I can't tell you of any other days prior to that moment but from that point on, my eyes and ears were wide open.

We lived in an old wooden house on a farm in Dos Palos, California. The morning fog made the air cool but not too cold. My dad was the boss. My mother seemed to be a child. She was afraid of my dad and tried to make her 4-foot-10-inch frame stand tall whenever he was around. She always seemed to be in defense mode when he was home. She stayed busy cleaning, cooking, ironing, and keeping us kids quiet. The responsibility fell on me to keep Little Leroy and Chief quiet when Dad got home or Mommy would get spanked and we would too. Usually Dad would just threaten my brothers and me, but he would quickly turn Mom over his lap and spank her.

I remember my daddy telling her that when he got home from work, his pants better all be pressed and hanging because he was going to the boxing matches after work. My mother would cry when he left because she didn't want him leaving us at night. My brothers decided that they would "help" Mommy so she would not be sad. They took my dad's pants into the closet and cut them with scissors so when he put them on they would be broken. I didn't know what they were doing in the closet; they were being quiet so Mom and I just let them play quietly. They did not realize what they truly did until my daddy put the pants on and one leg was missing. They did it to three pair of slacks. Well, their mission was accomplished that night. My dad didn't go out to the boxing match and my mother wasn't crying. When Dad wanted to know who did it, both my brothers pointed to me in unison as if they had rehearsed it. It was always easier for me to take the spanking than it was to witness my mother or brothers get placed over my dad's knee. Just hearing their anguish hurt my heart. A butt-whipping pain goes away, but the sight of someone you love hurting will stay with you much longer. Eyes are the windows of the soul, right? Early in my life I realized that I could feel the pain that others experienced when I looked into their eyes. I quietly took the punishment.

The next thing I remember was moving from the burning farm to San Jose. Now we were in a neighborhood where there were streetlights and sidewalks and a pony that pranced around the neighborhood. It was a Shetland pony with cowboy gear, and anyone who wanted to could sit on the pony and get a ride and have a picture taken while sitting on him. My mom split the cowboy gear up between the three of us: one wore the gun and holster, the other wore the cowboy hat, and the third wore the britches or chaffs. Mommy sat the three of us up on the pony and we rode the block like real cowboys. We should have had Indian gear on since we are Native Americans. But who cares when you are having so much fun? My mom and dad weren't arguing and they seemed to enjoy each other and us three kids. Perhaps my brothers cutting up my dad's slacks caused him to slow down and finally delight in the smart kiddos he was responsible for bringing into this world. Who knows why my parents were in such rare form but it was nice. I don't remember any other days after this one where we had a joyful time. This was it for a very long time.

Then came a new adventure in my valley of life. All that I can recall is "no more dad." It was just my mother, brothers, and me living with my grandmother Charli, who I am named after. I walked to kindergarten with other children in Hollister, California. I learned little songs like "Where Is Thumb Man?" and "Twinkle, Twinkle Little Star." My grandmother would teach me other songs even though she knew I would never get the words right. She just loved to hear my little voice making up words as I sang. She was really enjoying having her grandbabies around.

There was a specific night that I can remember vividly. My mother, grandmother, and Aunt D went out dancing. My grandmother had a cousin who was going to be our babysitter for the night. He was tall, quiet, and maybe a teenager or a little bit older. We will call him Dick. Dick was watching my two brothers and me that night as they all went dancing. We were not much to watch since the three of us were already asleep in one twin bed when he arrived. Dick came into the room where my brothers and I were sleeping and woke me up. He got me up out of the bed and told me to be very quiet so we wouldn't wake up my brothers. He took my hand and led me to my grandmother's room and asked me if I wanted a "7 up." I was five years old, I was thinking 7 up means soda pop, right? As he started to pull down his zipper, I made my way to the other side of my grandmother's bed because I was scared. A grip of fear flooded me like I felt when my dad was going to whip me. I was trapped between my grandmother's bed and the wall. All I could do was shrink to the floor and I covered my eyes like my daddy taught me to do when my brothers pulled down their zippers to go pee-pee. I was crying and knew something was very wrong. Why me in the bedroom? Why not my brothers who love soda pop? Luckily my grandmother's front door opened. Everyone had returned early. They were loud and drunk, but not so drunk that they didn't notice me and my cousin in my grandmother's bedroom. I was told to get back in bed and I heard, "Why are you up?"

The next thing I knew, my grandmother's home wasn't our home any longer. Kindergarten was over. No dad, no home. As I look back at that night in a dark scary cave along the path in my valley, there was definitely an angel watching over me.

Later on, my grandmother recalled that night as if it had happened yesterday. She told me that my mother was dancing with gangsters that night. Not gangsters like we know them today but gangsters like Al Capone. Those gangster types used to hang out in the Watsonville area where my grandmother liked to go dancing. She didn't want her daughters caught up in that lifestyle so she decided it was a good time to leave. My grandmother told me that leaving a bar or nightclub early was not something they normally did. They would dance and drink until the bars closed every time they went out and Dick knew it. Thank God He brought my family home early that night.

My mother was as pretty as the noonday sun and she knew it. Her petite size of 4'10", long red hair, and scattered freckles caused people to see the angel within her not realizing she was part Irish, part Native American, and part Mexican. She was definitely hot tempered and not at all angelic. At the local bars, they witnessed her hot temper. She would get on top of the bar, break a beer bottle, and say, "Come on with it" to anyone she perceived was being disrespectful. She could lure the men in like flies. She could get them to pay for all of her drinks and if they were lucky she would take one home with her, but it was going to cost them something. Don't let her stature fool you: she was not as sweet and innocent as she appeared.

She got her rent paid, groceries on the table, and nice outfits for the next round of events. I can remember several times when our mother had us walk with her on the streets of San Joaquin to shop and we would see some of the men who spent nights with her. Very innocently, the three of us would say, "Hi, Uncle Bobby," "Uncle Ralph," "Uncle Juan," or so many other "uncles" who came over. Of course we didn't know they were bed partners. On the streets they acted like they didn't hear us or see us. Maybe they didn't recognize us because they had their wives and children with them on those embarrassing moments. To all these uncles we were just strange children. They didn't know that Lupe was our mother. They all thought she was only our babysitter. After all, who wants to date a woman with three kids except for a piece of booty! If she looked like she was poor and babysitting around the clock, perhaps some man would cough up some cash and help her out; or maybe he would marry her petite self because she was so poor and worked so hard and was so beautiful, plus she was the best dancer in the bar scene. Anyway you would never know she was our mom as we were not allowed to call her "Mommy." We had to call her "Lupe."

Somehow she was able to pull off this ruse for a couple of years until she became an alcoholic and would forget where she left us children. If someone found out she was our mother and didn't like it, she would gladly tell them to "get the 'you know what' out of her house." She didn't care who you were or who you were with, she had business to tend to. She would always say, "If you don't like the peaches, don't shake my tree!" or "No money, no honey." In other words, her beautiful body and time were worth your money; if the three kids bothered you, get on down the ramp you tramp because Momma's got bigger fish to fry!

Sometimes, my mother would prepare for her "guests" and position my little brothers under her bed, not so they could hear or hide because she was babysitting us, but so they could rob the man when his pants fell to the ground. My brothers' instructions were to take the man's wallet out of the pocket, take all the cash, put the wallet back into the same pocket, and put the pants back where the man dropped them. The men never knew they lost their money at Lupe's bed; they thought they lost it before they got to her house. They were all intoxicated when they reached her house so they never did find out. The men who ended up at my mother's house had every intent to screw her, but her intent was to screw them first by taking their money out of their pockets. The smell of stale booze, cigarettes, sweat, and the aftermath of many men's aftershaves and colognes plus my mother's favorite perfume 'Tabu' was like a cloud that you couldn't escape. Add to that cloud the smell of urine from the little boys who peed their pants because they were under the bed so long—it was a scent that lingers. That is a hard smell to forget.

It actually seemed better when I was locked up in a closet for days at a time with just my little brothers. Mom would leave water in a bucket or a jar or whatever she could find and a loaf of bread. I clearly remember the loaf of bread that she would leave in the closet because it had a picture of a little blonde girl with a whirly, blue and white checkered dress I always wished I could be that happy little girl with that beautiful dress. The only light and warmth that would penetrate through the darkness of the closet was when the sunlight peeked through the windows and warmed up the closet through the slats. We would hunch under a sheet or under a pile of dirty clothes so we could stay warm. We were just little people who didn't know any better, but we sure knew that if we made a peep in that closet, the boogieman would come and chop off our heads or eat us. The boogieman didn't show up, but our mother would eventually come back and scare us to death. She had a bad habit of leaving us alone while she went out. Nine times out of ten, our mother locked us inside the closet. Sometimes though, we intentionally didn't go home, hiding outdoors until she left, then we had full rein of the house. But it actually felt safer and warmer inside a closet. When she got home, she would scare us by scratching on the window screens. Most of the time she was drunk before she left the house so we never got tucked into a bed or kissed at night. She didn't seem to care what happened to us. But she did care if she could hear us.

She seemed to take most of her frustrations out on my brother Chief, the middle child. I don't know why, but I learned early on to stand in front of him before she threw something like a plate of spaghetti. She would hit him square in the face and laugh if I didn't get between them in time. I cried. He cried. All I could think of at that time was that one day I was going to take my brothers and run away. Anywhere was better than with this awful mother.

I also learned that if we fell asleep somewhere, the time would pass faster and I could protect them for a little while. But why didn't anyone see us and why didn't anyone call the police and tell on her? I thought that maybe everyone lived the same way we did. Maybe children were little people who couldn't or shouldn't say anything because they had big people calling the shots. I would have to grow up before I could change anything because then I would have power like they did. Just the thought of being left in closets, sleeping under piles of dirty clothes, hearing scratching on screen doors, and hearing her calling Chief's name to the windows only to scare him and us to death still brings tears to my eyes.

She only locked us in the closet and left us alone when she didn't need us. Sometimes she needed us to help her with things. I didn't realize how we were helping her until I got older. It wasn't until I was in my thirties that I realized my mother was boosting or stealing the layers of clothes she was wearing when we would go out in public. She looked so innocent, so who would do such a thing when shopping with their little children? I wish you could have seen my face when I realized my mother was a booster. Wow, I was an accessory to crimes at the age of five and my brothers at ages three and four! I am sure the courts knew we were her pawns and were not responsible. My mother didn't send us to the stores to shoplift. We learned how to do that all by ourselves. We learned by watching her. She didn't give us pennies to buy bubble gum, but her men would give us change so we would leave the house. One of the best things I can remember about these times was when we could get outdoors so we could run to the little neighborhood grocery stores and take that change to buy bubble gum.

The men knew that when they came over to bring a bottle of booze to saturate our mother's taste, then they could have their way with her. I learned early it was better to be outside in the neighborhood than to be locked up in a closet for days. Have you ever eaten bread with butter and sugar? It tasted so good, especially when you're hungry and sometimes that was the only food in the house. We learned real quick how to eat without paying at these two little neighborhood stores. We would open the bread bags and take a few slices, put our fingers in peanut butter jars if we could open them and finally get to eat. No one in the store knew because we watched each other's back as one did the devious deed. My brothers were good at taking men's money out of their pockets and putting the wallets back, so they were already professionals when it came to being sneaky.

I thought we were getting away with it but the storeowners were suspicious and called the police because the three of us went shopping for food without our mother. Why would three children under six years old be in the stores without their mother? Why were they hungry? And who were these dirty kids? We became the neighborhood rascals and started gaining a police record. We also got really quick at running and slipping through people's knees and hands; plus we found hiding places where we could lay low until dark with a whole loaf of bread and a whole jar of peanut butter. We learned to put bubble gum in our pockets before we paid for the *one* piece. We had to survive. We had to eat. We had to sleep under dirty laundry. We had to hide. We had to be quiet. We had no one to care for us or show love. What is love anyway? We didn't choose this valley. We were set in it and we had to learn to make the best of it or literally die. The three of us were close—we had to be. Being close meant being warm and being fed!

Before long, the storeowners realized we weren't thieves—just hungry children. They would have a brown bag filled with peanut butter sandwiches, a treat, and something for us to drink. When they saw us at their entrance, their faces were calm but their demeanors were sad. They would beckon us to come in and take their surprises but they would also notify the authorities that we were back. The police were smart and didn't show up where we could see them. They would wait until we led them home after dark and they would follow us. After dark was a safe time to return home, so that's when we would go. Our mother would be gone to the bars by then and she wouldn't be around to hurt Chief. We were cute little rascals. Our clothes were dirty—we were dirty—but we laughed, played, and imagined things like eating at a table that wasn't there or hugging each other as if we knew what love was. We had each other and the three of us were content as long as we were together.

We started actually getting arrested by the police when we were found on the streets, or at least this is what we thought was happening. The police picked us up and we went to receiving homes in the local area of San Joaquin, our hometown. But it didn't seem bad, rather it seemed good since we were kept together and we were fed at a real table with hot food several times a day, given warm baths and clean clothes. Each of us had a bed with a pillow and warm blankets. People hugged us and we felt wanted. We had backyards to play in with swings, teeter-totters, slides, and toys. Then just when we got comfortable and felt like this was the life that the little girl on the bread bag lived, we had to get dressed in other clothes because we couldn't take those clothes home to our mother's. They were for the next children who would visit, however, the clothes on our backs were ours to keep.

After several receiving homes and the many chances that the courts gave our mother, she figured out which neighbors and other people were turning her in as an unfit mother. It was the neighbors across the hall who could hear us in the closet. It was the owners of grocery stores. It was neighbors who were complaining about those little rascals diving in their garbage cans and leaving a mess. It was also patrons at the local bars calling the cops because three little children were being left in the car for hours at a time with no food or water while their mother was in the bar drinking. Believe it or not, all those people had the courage to report an injustice. It was a blessing to be arrested or better yet rescued from an evil world of chaos, degradation, and many forms of filth. The courts of San Joaquin were the rescuers and my mother's role was evil. The shadows of darkness in our valley seemed like Hell when we didn't know where we were or who would offer a hand to lift us up!

My mother wised up and decided that leaving us at home was no longer an option. She would pay for a babysitter because her drinking wasn't the problem: it was her being an unfit mother. She couldn't risk having us picked up again or she would lose her welfare check for the three of us. All she had to do was relocate us while she left for days at a time or whenever she went to dance and party. The best babysitter yet was the local movie theater. She let us know that we were on our way to a castle like the one in the *Jack and the Beanstalk* book, the only story she ever read to us. This theater was that very castle where the "good giant" lived and we would be safe in there. She would sit us down in the theater chairs with our laps full of popcorn, candy, and a soda—what a treat! The first and my favorite movie was *Ben Hur*. Ben Hur was a man after my own heart. He was someone who rescued people, and I think he talked about Jesus or the man from Nazareth if I remember correctly. The way I remember Ben Hur was that he helped people, people of little stature like my brothers and me. I wanted to marry him when I got older. He was a king in my eyes and maybe a man like that would find my brothers and me and rescue us forever! My brothers were still little, so taking them to the bathroom, getting them back to our seats, making sure they had something to eat, and keeping them quiet so we didn't get thrown out was my responsibility.

Somehow we pulled it off until closing. The ushers were not responsible for getting us to our mother. It was my responsibility to assure them when they locked us outdoors in the dark that our mother was right around the corner waiting to pick us up. I don't know what time the San Joaquin Theater closed but it was surely after the town closed, as there was no life on the streets, barely any lights on, no cars, no people, and no mother for sure. She must have forgotten about us or was totally drunk somewhere. We couldn't sit on the corner of the street all night or some boogieman might find us and kill us; or the police would arrest us and our mother would kill us. We were hungry and we were so cold that we were shivering. Most times the three of us could huddle and get warm but in the midst of this fog and the cold air, there wasn't a huddle strong enough to keep us from crying and wishing our mother would show up. She didn't. The police first heard us as they drove their beat then they saw us huddled and crying … it was Lupe's kids again. They first put us into their car to get us warm and then they fed us whatever they had on hand. Later we woke up in a safe, warm place and then ended up in a courtroom with our mom.

11

I remember this particular court proceeding because the judge wouldn't let us sit with our mother. The judge ordered my mother to sit in the front so she could see her better and wanted to make sure our mother heard every word. I don't think our mother had a clue that the judge's clerk was my grandmother's niece, Alicia. But the judge knew of my grandmother's daughters—especially my mother and her value as a mother: none! The judge seemed to be on the side of my brothers and me. She didn't have a kind face when she looked toward my mother, yet she seemed to crack a bit of a smile when she looked toward us children. She struck the gavel hard and loud. Maybe she was trying to scare my mother or wake her up in case she was still drunk or hungover. It got her attention and my little mother stopped fidgeting and stood up as if at attention. This day in court she dressed like an old woman, without makeup just like she dressed when she was cleaning house. Yes, my mother did clean the house and when she did cook, she was a great cook. We stood beside a policeman and this time we couldn't walk to our mom. We had to stand next to the police officers and not engage in cuddles or conversation with our mom. It was as if she had a disease or there was a restriction because she might cause us harm. I don't know why, but I am sure my mother got a clear picture of who was in power this time. This was what the picture would look like forever if my mother didn't pay attention to the judge.

"Court is in session!"

My mother was standing at attention as Alicia handed the judge a piece of paper. The judge wanted to know if Lupe was in court. Of course she knew she was in court as she ordered my mother to stand before her, but she wanted to hear my mother say, "Yes, Your Honor." The judge told my mother, from what I recall, "This is your last chance as you are found to be an unfit mother; your children will remain as wards of the court today, unless you follow my rules and the rules of this court. Do you understand?"

"Yes, Your Honor."

The judge continued, "These children will attend Catechism weekly, and as I understand from my clerk, your mother is active in the local

Catholic Church, is that correct? Plus, the nuns have assured the court that they will keep a watchful eye on these children and also keep an account with this courtroom if the children miss a single Catechism. If the children miss a single Catechism, they will be picked up, put in foster homes, and never returned to you. Do you understand?"

My mother understood and agreed. We went home with her and my mother followed the rules for a while.

This doesn't mean that my mother stopped her bad habits. She had a steady boyfriend, Juan. He seemed to love my mother and tolerated us. She appeared happy. She and Juan spent lots of time in bed cuddling and my mother cooked, cleaned, stopped taking us to stores to boost, and no more hiding under the bed. We attended Sacred Heart Catholic Church. Sacred Heart was just a few blocks away from my elementary school. Life was good, but the local nuns gave my brothers and I the impression we were on their hit list. Not that they hit us, but when all the other children got pats on the back or head or maybe even a hug, the nuns would not touch my brothers or me. It was obvious. Even the other children noticed. Children can be cruel. They would lean toward us and sniff to see if we smelled bad; or say things such as, "You have cooties!" What are cooties? Whatever they are, it was like we were contagious and the other children kept clear of us. The whole congregation at church knew my grandmother, but they also knew our mom, and our mom was known for sleeping around, which could bring bugs, fleas, or maybe cooties into the church if anyone touched us. There was nothing I could do about it except to do as I was told: keep to ourselves, pay attention, say the Hail Marys and Our Fathers, and repent with the Rosary wrapped around my little hands.

The stories I learned in Catechism of Jesus were sad—Him hanging on a cross with nails in His hands and feet, the crown of thorns, and people spitting on Him and beating Him. It was so sad and terrible. And they had pictures and statues of Him everywhere inside the church showing His sad face. All Jesus wanted was to love people and for us to love Him back. They taught us that He died for us, He bled for us. I didn't understand if He was so powerful, why did He have to do this? Why did He have to go? If He was a spirit, could He come and sit with us now? Did He see us now? Did He still love us, after all these bad things happened to Him? One thing I did understand for sure: when I took my Holy Communion, He would see me accept Him as my Savior and my Father. I wanted Him to know, "I believe in you, Lord, and I accept you, forever."

Some time had passed after court and now I was turning seven years old and preparing to receive my first Holy Communion. That special day came and I will remember it for the rest of my life. It was the day when my family was so excited for me. They dressed me in a beautiful white dress, a white veil, dainty white shoes with white ruffly socks, and the Rosary wrapped around my hands. My beautiful long hair reaching down to my waist. I finally looked like the little blonde girl on the bread bags. My mother and her friends told me I was beautiful. The nuns had us rehearse several times before the big day. I knew exactly what Jesus was expecting of me: to believe in Him and trust him because He died for me! The church was packed. People were getting ready for picnics and barbecues afterward. Their little square black cameras were taking pictures of us all. Those of us taking our Holy Communion had certain rules to obey. First, keep our eyes and face forward. No waving or turning our heads once we walked into the sanctuary. Keep our hands folded and holding your Rosary. No talking or any silliness. After all, God was watching and the nuns were too. Take our positions, boys to the front row, right side, and girls to the front row, left side. We were all to kneel together and wait to receive His body and blood, which was bread and wine. I was ready to receive and knew this was the beginning of a new life; little did I know I was still in the valley of the shadows of darkness. This, however, was the turning point which would mark me for the rest of my life.

I was scared, excited, committed, and ready for whatever Jesus had for me. I believed in Him then at the age of seven as I do now and I don't regret one moment. When the priest blessed the bread and wine and began to serve them to each child, I opened my mouth wide and gladly, but nearly threw up with the Blood of Christ. It wasn't like any grape juice I had ever tasted! It tasted like blood—like the blood I had tasted when I had a small cut on my finger! What was going on? I didn't move my face, but I did move my eyes to the left and the right to see if any other children were reacting to the grape juice. No, just me. Then the flesh of Jesus, the little piece of bread, was next. Again, I opened my mouth ready to receive the bread, but that was no bread. It tasted like actual flesh! I had tasted it before, too—the skin on my fingers when I peeled them. But now it was Jesus' blood and Jesus' flesh. Again same routine: I didn't move my face, just my eyes to see if other girls and boys were experiencing this phenomenon, but it appeared that no one except me tasted the blood and flesh. God apparently meant this profound experience just for me on that day. I immediately felt like a marked child, one who was different—one who was unlike the others. Perhaps that was what the nuns knew about me, perhaps that was why none of them would touch or love my brothers or me. There was something wrong with me, I thought. Then all of us children taking our Holy Communion stood up and marched outside the church to our families. I excited the chapel doors, our hands still folded, our faces and eyes fixed forward. As I stepped outside of the church doors, a nun reached out to me and put her hand on my left shoulder, my face still fixed forward I was feeling very blessed at that moment because a nun touched me and she said something which prepared me for the rest of my life, "Mija (Spanish for "my daughter"). When she said Mija, I looked up at her, "you'll know who your Father is because they will treat you the same way they treated your Father."

I believe with every ounce of my being that it was not a nun who touched my shoulder that day. I believe it was an angel that Jesus sent to prepare me for the shadows of darkness in which I would begin to walk that same day as my Holy Communion. During my Holy Communion, I vowed my life to Christ. I was surely touched by an angel. That was the day that my life changed forever. If it wasn't for that word from an angel dressed like a nun, all the setups of where I had been before that moment, and the precise timing, I would never have survived. God doesn't make mistakes. We do. I didn't choose my parents or their ages when I was born; God did. He knew the plans He had for me and what I had to endure so He could prepare me for the plans He set before me. Yes I was a marked child, and I knew who my Father was because they treated me just like they treated Jesus.

After that nun touched me and gave me that message, I saw that there was a police car and a Department of Social Services car waiting for me at the bottom of those chapel steps. We did not get to celebrate like the other children and we did not get to live with our mother anymore. We were now wards of the court going to a German family, who had German ways. We were children who had been thrown away and they had to feed, clothe, and take care of the three of us. We were children whose parents were known alcoholics, a whore, tramp, unhealthy, and probably had cooties or whatever bugs and sicknesses come with "those kind!"

The Bible says, "Yea, though I walk through the valley of the shadow of death, I will fear no evil." Yeah, right. That wasn't happening. I was afraid! My brothers were standing with my mother. She was standing on the stair steps on the other side of this nun (the angel) and I wasn't able to touch my mother. They had to pry my brothers out of her hands. No longer did the courts see her as a fit mother and now our new life began. Timing is everything—God's timing is perfect! That nun, at that moment with those words, was precisely the right moment, because within the next hour our Hell began. I was scared to death for the next seven years in that foster home. Scared to death!

LIFE IN FOSTER CARE

"But you, God, see the trouble of the afflicted; you consider their grief and take it in hand. The victims commit themselves to you; you are the helper of the fatherless."

PSALM 10:14 NIV

T he police were coordinating our every move as we were ushered into the Social Service car which was parked right behind the police car. When the three of us were tucked in the backseat and the car door was shut, the police pulled away and the woman driver began talking to us. She was a big woman with a gentle voice, trying to soothe the upset children, letting us know we were going to our new home and our mother was no longer able to take care of us. Our father was nowhere to be found. We would be happy because the people we were going to live with wanted three children and they had a big farm with animals. We would have our own beds and bedrooms, plus other children to play with. But why today? Why not after our Holy Communion celebration? I don't know, but I am certain that nun knew.

The drive to wherever we were going seemed to be never ending, but it was only about five miles, near the San Joaquin airport, where the farm was. Our home was the only home for miles, a large white home with a basement, four bedrooms, one bathroom, a front yard, chicken coop, a cow named Daisy, a hog, dogs, cats, a big kitchen, plus a dining room and a porch. When we pulled up to the backdoor entrance, a metal tub with a hose sticking in it was outside the four or five steps leading to the covered porch. A tall, slender, white woman greeted us at the car and asked the driver for our clothes. She wasn't very happy with the answer that we had none. But she said she would make do. She didn't lead us into her home, but as soon as the social service woman pulled away, she told us to undress to our underwear so she could rinse us off. We didn't understand, so she quickly grabbed my baby brother Little Leroy and took off all his clothes except his underwear. We undressed too, and she took the water hose and sprayed us with cold water, gave us a towel, and told us to share it. We did. As I was drying my brothers off, she immediately told me, "Stop!" They could dry themselves as they were big boys and that's not what she told us to do.

Once we were dry, she led us into the interior porch that had her wringer washer and clothesline. She had another scrubbing for us without our underwear and we put all of our clothes in her wringer as we stood naked. She draped a sheet around each one of us and told us to stand still. Dad would be in to cut my brothers' hair. She went inside the house and retrieved an empty orange carrot bag. She had a pair of scissors and told me she was going to cut my hair and send it to my mother so our mother wouldn't forget about us. She then took my long locks and put them up in a ponytail and cut my hair to the back of my scalp. My brothers' hair was shaved. Then she brushed off the hair from the sheets outside and had us stand still until she handed us clothes to put on. She talked about the rules and obeying her every word.

"Children were to be seen and not heard."

We wanted our mommy and wanted to know if we were going home. Did we do something wrong? The police took us, put us into a car, now we are in this home in the middle of nowhere. I couldn't have figured a way off that farmland if I wanted to. It was a huge field. I had never seen anything like it—miles and miles of grass or hay or whatever they were growing in that field. My mom was going to be heartbroken if she got that carrot bag with my hair in it. My mom would think I was dead. Why would my mother forget about us? Weren't we going to see her again? Oh, my goodness – my heart ached and I was filled with anxiety!

Before I get too far into my life in foster care and introduce you to the ways of my foster mom, I need to preface it by saying that humans are flawed beings. Not everyone who professes to be a Christian grasps the redemptive love of Christ and the personal relationship He offers. Some are misguided. The Bible says, *"Even Satan disguises himself ... therefore it is not surprising if his servants also disguise themselves as servants of righteousness, whose end will be according to their deeds"* (2 Corinthians 11:14–15 NASB)

So we followed this woman into the next room, the kitchen. It smelled so good. She was already preparing dinner and we hadn't had breakfast or lunch, so the kitchen was the best place to be at this moment. At least that was what we thought until she told us that we had to wait for dinnertime because lunch was already over for today. We were dismayed and hungry but alert to her rules. She knew my name and told us to look at her when she spoke or called our names. We were looking straight up at her while she had us sit on a long wooden bench at the kitchen table. She walked to the refrigerator and picked up a bell she rang and said, "Whenever you hear this bell ring, it is time to eat. No ifs, ands, or buts. When you hear that bell, you drop whatever you are doing, wash your hands, get to the table, and sit exactly where you are sitting."

Then she said, "Charli, when you hear this bell in the morning, you get up and come to this broom closet and pick one of these straps and meet me in the bathroom. Do you understand?" I nodded my head but she wasn't having any head nods. She wanted a "Yes, ma'am." "Yes, ma'am," I said in a low voice. She wanted me to speak up louder, so again I said, "Yes, ma'am." She told us to get up and follow her to the bathroom where we would meet each morning before breakfast with one of the leather straps. She wanted to know if we understood her and we all nodded our heads. She quickly corrected our head nods again to a "Yes ma'am." We were obedient and we followed her to our various bedrooms. My brothers shared a bedroom with our new parents' teenage son and I shared a room with their adopted daughter. The three of us had our own beds, dresser, and blankets. As soon as we walked to our rooms, she immediately took the pillows off our beds and told us we wouldn't be needing pillows. I guess they were for show not for comfort. Funny how her daughter and son got pillows, but maybe it was because they didn't have cooties or perhaps because they had a real mom and dad and we didn't deserve such a treat. Who knows? Later on she told us that a pillow could cause our necks and spine to grow crooked. Really? Then why did her son and daughter have pillows?

That evening when the bell rang, we ran for dinner but we forgot to wash our hands. That was the beginning of being pulled up from the table by our ears and taken to the bathroom to wash our hands. We never forgot to wash our hands again. That pulling-the-ears stuff worked. But we still couldn't eat the food in front of us because she had to read a little story from *Our Daily Word* and then she would pray or read the prayer which was printed on the little book. That was the ritual every evening, then we could eat. We would clean our plates, every last drop of food, like it or not. It was cool to sit at the table with everyone, but no talking, no slouching, no coughing, and no getting up until everyone was done. There were lots of rules, lots of things to remember; but she said the one thing we needed to forget was our mother. She said we needed to forget her because we would never see her again, and as for our father, he was a loser and didn't deserve to have kids.

Just like "mom" said, she rang the morning bell promptly at seven and I ran to the broom closet to impress our new mom and did as I was told: picked out a leather strap and met her in the bathroom with my brothers. She was waiting for us in the bathroom, sitting on the toilet seat. It was a small bathroom with a small tub, a small sink, and the toilet. It was better for one person, not four of us at a time. That's the moment that another chapter of Hell began.

The leather strap was to beat the devil out of us each morning so we didn't grow up to be like our parents. We had to bend over the bathtub together with nothing on but our underwear and she whipped us from the back of our necks to the back of our knees, and if we screamed we got more stripes just like Jesus. I finally understood what the nun meant, "You will know who your Father is, because they will treat you just like they treated Him." Obviously Jesus is my Father, because they were whipping us just like they whipped Jesus. But this was just the beginning of seven years of torture. Who would think that the police authorities would allow adults to do such things to children and take us from our mother to bring us to a home of torture? I can't count the times I had to watch my brothers being tortured. If I dropped a tear, the three of us had to dress down and get that leather belt whipping. You know, I didn't mind the morning beatings much after five years. It was still painful, but we had no control over the inevitable. We had to bend over and hope she wouldn't hit us so much or so long. She seemed to enjoy these moments in the bathroom. I can still see the sullen look on my baby brothers' eyes after all these years. Little Leroy wouldn't shed a tear. He would just bite his lip, shrug his shoulders, and keep on trucking as if he didn't feel a thing. But Chief and I still cried our hearts out and I kept thinking surely Jesus is our Father because they treat us the same way they treated Jesus.

Let me paint a picture for you of these years. Our daily schedule at Mrs. H's began at 7:00 AM. We walked to the bathroom with our underwear on and bend over the bathtub. We waited for Mrs. H to give us our daily whipping. Then we had morning chores before breakfast. My responsibility was to make lunches for all of us children and set the breakfast table. After breakfast I had to wash the dishes, dry them, and put them away. Then I would get dressed for school. I made sure our beds were made, our bedroom clean, and our dirty clothes were in the hamper. I would make sure our hair was combed, our teeth brushed and checked by Mrs. H before we left for school. We had to be sure to catch the bus but if we missed it, we had to run to school. When we got home from school, we changed from our school clothes into our everyday clothing and shoes. This was the easy part. The hard part was coming home from school not knowing what kind of madness we would have to endure. My brothers and I became bedwetters. That was unforgivable and for sure we would be whipped if our beds were wet. We quickly learned how to sneak a towel and put it on our soiled sheets, and then the flat sheet on top of our quilt. We made sure there wasn't a wrinkle on it and it looked good as new. However, that didn't last long. Mrs. H tore back the blankets and sheets and the large urine circles were exposed in all three of our beds. Of course our hearts beat harder and faster and our stomachs were nauseous because we could feel a cloud of pain approaching us. It was inevitable. We didn't have to walk down the hall to the bathroom. She had us bend over the bed and put our nose on the wet mattress or sheet and we got our beatings in our bedroom. After our beating it was time to strip the beds, wash the plastic sheets that covered our mattresses, and put on clean sheets that I had ironed. I became clever about wetting my bed. Knowing I would have an accident, I started stealing towels and putting them under my butt when I went to bed, so if I peed my bed my sheets wouldn't be wet, just the towel. However I had to hide those pee towels somewhere so my mission was to steal three towels for the three of us kids, and my brothers' mission was to hide the towels somewhere. They found the perfect hiding spot under the house. Now we could only hide so many towels from the linen closet. Whenever Mrs. H was washing clothes, I would put one or two towels in the washing machine not considering Mrs. H knew exactly what laundry was in the washing machine. I became a liar because of fear and whenever Mrs. H wanted to talk to me, I knew she was on a discovery mode and the discovery better sound honest and wise or someone was getting tortured seriously! The washing machine was an old wringer machine and each individual item in the washing machine had to be hand-processed through the wringer. Of course a towel going through the ringer was noticeable. Lucky for me Mrs. H got tired of pushing and pulling long towels through the ringer, so she taught me how to do it. This gave me a sense of freedom in one respect because I knew I could put more towels in the washing machine and the pee towels would not be discovered because I was handling the laundry. We did have a dryer but it was used for only small items.

Everything larger than a hand towel was hung up outside and, truthfully speaking, I loved hanging the laundry. When my little brothers would have a pee-pee accident, our foster mother would pull my little brothers' pants down and place a rubber band around their private parts or tie a thread or string around their private parts to the point of drawing blood. I could hardly swallow. Attempting to hold a tear back was impossible. So we got more beatings like Jesus did. Surely Jesus was my Father because Mrs. H treated us just as if she was the one who whipped Jesus. Why did she do these things? Because we became bedwetters and she was going to cut those things off or make us regret we peed the beds. That 'private parts' torture didn't work so other tactics were tried, like taking our wet sheets and hanging them over our heads in front of neighbors' homes. Apparently Mrs. H thought humiliation would work but the neighbors only felt sorry for the three of us.

The times when Mrs. H had us stand on the edge of our street with our heads covered with our pee-stained sheets was not only humiliating but the smell was horribly pungent, especially when the sun beat down on us. Of course, no one in the neighborhood would miss seeing three children with sheets over their heads standing on the edge of their street. Even though we cried the entire time we were under the sheets, it was better than a belt whipping. People who passed by us in their cars, bicycles, or walking didn't make fun of us. They would slow down and we could sense their shame for us, not against us. However, they didn't act on our behalf or become our friends. They seemed to distance themselves even more. Who wants to become friends with damaged goods? Only Jesus could love us like we were. I knew He must have cried for us. The shortest scripture in the Bible is *"Jesus wept."* (John 11:35 ESV) The Bible also says, *"And God will wipe away every tear from their eyes."* (Rev. 7:17 NKJV); as well as *"You have taken account of my wanderings; Put my tears in Your bottle; Are they not in Your book?"* (Psalm 56:8 NASB). I believe this means He looks at us in every moment and in every event and doesn't miss a tear.

After so many years of whippings, there was no spot on our backs that had natural flesh which wasn't some shade of blue, purple, green, or gray, between the back of our necks and our knees. We were children living in the shadows of death during this journey in our valley—and death is what I wished for many times especially when my brothers were tied to anthills or locked in a basement of utter darkness without me. Mrs. H knew it hurt me more to hear my brothers cry than to be with them in the darkness. I hated her. The ant mound took me over the edge. I decided when I washed dishes that night that I would sneak a butcher knife into my bed and get up while everyone was asleep and stab her in the heart. Her adopted daughter didn't like her either and wanted her dead too, so she was going to keep watch for me that night. I was scared, but not so scared that I wouldn't stab her; rather, I was afraid that she might wake up while I attempted to stab her. Well, the butcher knife plot didn't work, because when I approached my foster mother's bedroom my foster sister cried out, "Mom! Mom! Charli's going to kill you!" Boy, I ran back to my bedroom and threw the knife in the dirty clothes basket near the bathroom door and pretended as though I was fast asleep making Patches look like a liar. My brothers knew I was planning to kill "Mom" and rescue us so they played along and acted like Patches had fabricated a complete lie. She was repeatedly caught in lies, so Mom didn't do anything except tell her to go back to bed. People who lie are never believed; they are like the little boy who cried wolf. Thankfully God didn't allow my murder scheme to succeed but from that time on, I knew I couldn't trust my foster sister with any secrets.

The weather was usually pleasant in central California, and there was always a breeze near the walnut trees where our clotheslines stood. The hardest part of the laundry was hanging the sheets, but I learned to fold them in half before putting them on the clothesline. That way when they dried they were more effortless to fold and easier to iron. I remember having three clotheslines and placing each item in an organized manner so when I brought the clothes in, they were pretty much separated. I realize it may be difficult to understand why this organized process was so important to me, but I had to stay out until all the laundry was off the clothesline. Without assistance, this task often wasn't completed until after dark. Unless there was a full moon, it was very dark since we lived where there were no streetlights. I wasn't given a flashlight so I became fearful of the dark. I learned to do things and chores right the first time so I didn't get punished at the end of the day, plus it gave me power over the darkness.

We grew up in that home working when we got up before we went to school, and working when we got home from school, working every day in the summer too, except for Sundays. God said rest on Sunday and so we rested—just normal duties like setting the table, taking out the trash, feeding the animals, and making our beds. On Sundays we ate fried chicken, mashed potatoes, corn on the cob, and a dessert; but I never had a day off from having to rub Mom's feet while she sat in her rocking chair. That was my nightly duty, and I mean nightly. It didn't matter if it was Christmas or birthdays, I was at her feet until it was bedtime. Bedtime meant that my brothers and I would have to kneel at her chair and say the "now I lay me down to sleep" prayer. This was our routine even when we were too sick to go to school. And God forbid if we threw up in the kitchen because we would have to mop it up and ingest it. Mrs. H thought that would teach us not to throw up in our eating place. There were a few times when I had to take my little hands to clean the mess off the table and consume it. To this very day I still have fingernail marks on my arms where I was pinched to the point of scars, because I heaved or vomited. It made her sick and I should have known better!

When I was in second or third grade and still living with Mrs. H, there was a little girl who came to our school. She always wore dirty clothes and her blonde hair was never combed or brushed. She always looked like she had just rolled right out of bed. At least my hair was always brushed and my clothes were clean. She was skinny and shy. No one wanted to play with her; she was like me in that regard. But she wouldn't even play with me—the other reject. My heart hurt for her because I could feel her pain. The fact is I have always believed that I am a daughter of Jesus; so if Jesus could do miracles and talk to God, surely

I should or could ask for divine intervention. Silently, I asked Jesus to help her, please; and would He tell me what I could do to help her. Every day I saw her and my heart wanted to reach out and give her some love, but she didn't get close to anyone. She seemed to blend in with the walls.

One evening when I was ready for bed, I sensed the Lord was trying to tell me something about that little girl. I stopped to listen. What I heard the Lord instruct me to do was to take some detergent, put it in a plastic sandwich bag, and mix it with water when I got to school. I was to tell her that Jesus wanted me to wash her hair with it. I obeyed. She was ready, willing, and accepting. It was right before the school bell rang. I remember washing her hair and trying to comb it with my fingers and dry it with paper towels. It was shiny, straight, and beautiful. From that day forward, she turned into another little popular blonde girl. Somehow, someway she was lifted up to a new level of life and never was the same old little sad girl; she was brand new. I knew it wasn't me who changed her. I knew it was my Father. I just obeyed Him and He performed a miracle. Maybe she knew of Jesus but never thought He loved her. Maybe in that simple act of kindness she realized that Jesus could see her and cared for her and she didn't need anything else except to know His loving touch just for a moment.

In hindsight, I see it as a visual image of how we are changed through the washing of Jesus blood. In Hebrews 10:22 NASB we read, *"Let us draw near with a sincere heart in full assurance of faith, having our hearts sprinkled clean from an evil conscience and our bodies washed with pure water."* If Jesus could change that little girl and make her brand new, He can do it for you! The Bible says, *"And such were some of you. But you were washed, you were sanctified, you were justified in the name of the Lord Jesus Christ and by the Spirit of our God."* (1 Corinthians 6:11 ESV) and *"Therefore, if anyone is in Christ, he is a new creation; old things have passed away; behold, all things have become new"* (2 Corinthians 5:17 NKJV). What would happen if you had a similar experience? Would you call it a miracle? This was one of my precious moments in hell and I definitely called it a miracle.

Another time when I was in fourth grade, everyone was assigned to write a story and read it out loud. I had to ask Jesus what to write about because I didn't play sports, dance ballet, play an instrument, or have any vacation stories. My life was filled with doom and gloom and telling people of something I did every day wouldn't be too exciting—especially if I told them that I had to rub my foster mother's feet every night. The kids would have laughed at me. But I could see the word 'Frito' as if I were looking in a mirror and the word was written on it. I asked Jesus, "What about Fritos?" I didn't know anything about Frito corn chips at the time because they weren't something we ever had the opportunity to delight in, ever. We three kids ate the same school lunch for seven years: An apple and a peanut butter and jelly sandwich or a ham sandwich. I know I should be grateful for that lunch because there were starving kids everywhere and we had a sack lunch every day. When we got a little bit older, my brothers and I got clever and started missing the school bus on purpose so we could walk to school and we started throwing our lunches onto the roof of a house that we passed along the way. We wondered if the lunches would still be there years later. We didn't even think that birds or animals would want them. We didn't care—we just kept the apple and threw the rest away. A bag of Fritos would have been like a banana split to us. I remember asking, "Okay, Lord, tell me about the Fritos." All I heard Him say was "magic Fritos." I had the title for my story. I wrote about the magic Fritos and how a single Frito was like a single wish. My fourth grade teacher asked me to read my story to the class and I got an A! Wow, I didn't have a life like the rest of the kids, but I had imagination; better yet, I had a Father who gave me precious moments.

That story made me a little popular in my class. Kids wanted to know if I wanted some of their Fritos. Sure! I wanted to taste a Frito, and from that day forward kids traded items in their lunches for my apple. I hadn't realized that apples were popular, but after seven years of eating them, they certainly were not popular with my brothers or me! Kids bartered their whole lunch; me, I wanted to eat in the cafeteria. Fat chance of that ever happening! The aromas from the cafeteria smelled even better than home cooking from Mrs. H.

My foster mom was an awesome cook and we didn't have a single evening meal without potatoes—one of Mr. H's absolute musts—potatoes anyway you want to serve them. I love potatoes anyway you want to serve them. Mrs. H cornered the market for home cooking. We never missed three square meals a day; after all, that was one of the proofs of knowing we were loved—three square meals, a bed to sleep in, a roof over our heads, and a beating every morning meant you were loved, didn't it? I never ever believed Mrs. H loved me, but I did believe Jesus was my Father; and I recall Jesus rarely having three square meals each day, a bed to sleep in, or roof over His head. He took each day as it was presented to Him. He told us not to worry about tomorrow because there were enough troubles in the day. If He fed the birds of the air and provided shelter for all His animals, He would surely take care of me.

TEEN YEARS

"The LORD is close to the brokenhearted and saves those who are crushed in spirit."

PSALM 34:18 NIV

When I was about thirteen years old, I had a choice to make. There was a lady who moved into the chicken coop turned studio apartment on our property. She knocked on our back porch door intending to complain to Mom about my brothers. I do not know what they did and I did not ask. Mom wasn't home when she knocked but I told her I would let her know when Mom got home. The more I thought about telling Mom that the neighbor wanted to see her, the angrier I got. I decided that if my brothers were going to get another beating for whatever this neighbor wanted to complain about, I would get a beating, too, because nothing my brothers may have done would deserve the torture they were going to experience. So I decided to knock on her door and let her know what trouble would arise if she spoke to our mom about my brothers.

I knocked, she answered. My conversation went something like this: "Ma'am, I don't know what my brothers did, but I know you hear us crying every morning. I'm sure you can hear us from our bathroom window. I know you hear it. What do you think she will do to my brothers and me when you tell her what they did? Is it worth us dying for? For God's sake, help us, please! Why won't anyone help us?" She was speechless.

I sat and waited for a knock at our door that afternoon, but that neighbor didn't show up when Mom got home. She never looked at me again. It was as if she was ashamed to look at me, but she was kind to my brothers and never complained about them. She tried to befriend them. I think that is called "mercy." I will never forget how I felt that day when I finally took a stand for my brothers. It was another part of me I didn't know existed. I felt empowered for the first time. I felt like God was answering my long time prayers by giving me the strength I had asked for. *"He gives strength to the weary and increases the power of the weak."* (Isaiah 40:29 NIV)

The other times I felt like I had some control in my life were when I climbed to the top of the walnut tree behind our house. I knew Mom couldn't get in the tree. I imagined that if I had supplies up on top of that tree, I might be able to live for a while. But then I thought that Mom would have ants climb the tree to get me or she would probably even go so far as to burn the tree down. So that safe feeling only lasted for a few minutes, but a few minutes were more than no minutes.

There were a few other times when I felt safe; like when my two brothers and I would get behind the two trunks which were kept in the closet of the bedroom I shared with my foster sister Patches. The three of us would sneak into the dark closet making sure not to turn the light on. We would sing "Jesus loves me, this I know." Every time we sang that song, we would cry our hearts out and the closet would light up with sprinkles of light. I knew my Father met us there and we would be refreshed or perhaps the word is "loved." I felt His love, His warmth, and His care. I knew He could see us. The closet was one of the few places that my brothers and I felt safe when we were living with our real mom too.

As soon as I would step out of that closet, thoughts of doubt and fear would run through my mind, just as I am sure happened to Peter when he stepped out of the boat and tried to walk on water with Jesus. He started sinking the minute he looked at the waves instead of keeping his eyes on Jesus.

It was hard, but the words that nun/angel spoke came back to me over and over. I knew who my Father was. I couldn't have endured the years of suffering if my head wasn't covered with the Blood of the Lamb, if I didn't know he was my friend and Savior! Life on earth was hard for Jesus too. He was born in a stable, sought after to be killed when He was just a baby; then beaten, shunned, and spat upon as an adult. I think of the children who go through pain and sorrow and never know that they are children of the most High God. They suffer not knowing why they are treated so harshly and without care, not considering that they are being treated just like their Father was. Why? Because of Satan. He doesn't want God to win our hearts and love. In this fallen world, unfit parents continue in their own selfish ways and turn their backs on their responsibilities. They serve themselves and do not serve God.

Satan tried his best to break my loving heart and spirit. He knew that if I survived this torture with the help of God, I could be a witness to others that no matter how dark the shadows of hell are, God can and will get you through them and create precious moments of light through the darkness. Yes, Satan has power, but not power over what Jesus already conquered—death! Satan wants us to give up and fall into place with the other lost souls. Since his way is easy, he tricks us with the temptations of that superficial fun for a moment and a false sense of control over our own lives. Way back in the garden, Eve thought she was in control for a moment, then all hell broke loose until Jesus set it straight. Yes, one man and one woman listened to that lying voice that said they could have all the knowledge and power of God. That lying voice still whispers to us, "You can have anything you want, just do it."

It is easy to give into selfishness and behaviors that damage and hurt others. All fun and games until one day you find yourself trapped. There is no one to pull you out of the hell you are in because you have pushed everyone else aside for your own gain or pleasures. Loneliness is a killer. That aloneness can envelop you and there is no way out but Jesus.

Without Him, you are lost. Satan comes to rob, steal, and destroy. He preys on the weak, on the lonely, on women and children. Are you any of these? I was all of these. I was a weak, lonely child, a woman who Satan tried to break. He especially tried to break my spirit when I was young.

There came a day when I was fourteen that I finally stopped wetting my bed and it was a memorable experience. I was allowed to sit in the dining room with visiting adults and family members for Thanksgiving dinner for the first time. After the table was set and all the fixings were on the table, Mom read the Daily Bread before we could eat. After she read it, we were all anxious to enjoy the feast. However, she stopped everyone and said, "Charli, excuse yourself and go to the bathroom. We don't want you to wet your pants like you do your bed."

I had to excuse myself after being horribly embarrassed, go cry in the bathroom, get my composure back, then get back to the table. That little show that Mom put on made my foster father very angry. He excused himself from the table because he had lost his appetite and he went and sat down in the living room to watch television. I had never seen Dad get mad before, especially not to the point of *not* eating. He never missed a meal. But when Mom embarrassed me, he was embarrassed for me. He helped me wash dishes that Thanksgiving and didn't say a word to me. He dried every dish and put all the dishes away for me. The next morning when Mom rang the bell for me and my brothers to meet her in the bathroom, Dad took the strap from my hands and told us to go back to our rooms. He took the belt and met Mrs. H in the bathroom and whipped her! We heard him ask, "How do you like it?" Mom screamed and cried and never talked to me again—not a word. That was punishment too. I hadn't done anything wrong. I was grateful though as I never got another spanking from her when Dad was home.

Sundays were relief days. My brothers and I learned where our biological mother was living and tried to run from church to her home and then back to church before the bus showed up to take us home. We were successful a few times. The three of us attended Sunday school every weekend at various churches depending on which churches sent buses out to pick up the children. We were Catholics when we moved from our mother's home. Then we became Nazarenes, Methodists, Lutherans, Baptists, Seventh Day Adventists, and finally, Presbyterians; all depending. All depending on which church sent out a bus. If the church had a Vacation Bible School during the summer, we went. As long as we weren't home we had relief from the wicked witch, plus we learned about Jesus. The stories were like rain from heaven. His mission in life was to love people and heal them and bring them hope. He was available everywhere, all the time within any of those denominations. And since He is everyone's Father, He would care and provide for those who have the faith of a mustard seed.

He wasn't a God who would kill this foster mother. He was the kind of God who would forgive her. Perhaps He was testing me to find out if I would forgive like He did. Or perhaps He allowed Mrs. H in my life to use the evil that was surrounding me and turn it around for His glory. That is exactly how I see it. As a child, I was reminded constantly that I was His child because every whipping reminded me of those words, "You will know who your Father is, because they will treat you just like they treated Him."

Stories like Sarah, Abraham's wife, who laughed at the messengers who told her she would have a child in her old age, were woven into my soul. A seeming impossibility—yet God kept His promise to Sarah and I knew He would keep His promise to me—to never leave or forsake me. However, I started praying and asking God, "Why me?" and, "Please take this cup from me" just like Jesus did when he talked to God in the Garden of Gethsemane before his crucifixion.

I knew with all my heart that He heard my prayers because peace would flow over me, especially when I hid in my closet behind those large trunks in the dark. My brothers and I would slip into my bedroom closet which I shared with Patches. We would wedge our little bodies behind the trunks and hanging clothes and softly sing "Jesus loves me this I know, for the Bible tells me so! Little ones to Him belong. They are weak, but He is strong. Yes, Jesus loves me! Yes, Jesus loves me. Yes,

Jesus loves me, the Bible tells me so!" We would cry our hearts out and then be flooded with a peace which was beyond understanding—peace along with hope, joy, and relief. I felt this closet was like the burning bush for Moses. It was almost like sacred ground because we met Jesus there! I knew that whatever we were enduring in our early years, God would turn it around for His glory. I didn't know when, why, or how; but I knew that as Daniel survived the lions' den, and Shadrach, Meshach and Abednego survived the raging fire, I would survive too! Ever since that nun put her hand on me and told me I would know who my father was, I knew that I would survive. Every single day for seven years we survived the wrath of Mrs. H. Disclosing all the details might break the strongest reader, yet there is light at the end of this story. Keep reading.

I will never forget the morning my bed was covered with blood. I didn't have a clue. I thought the back of my legs or back were bleeding from the belt whippings, so I tried to see behind me in the bathroom mirror. I stood on the toilet and bathtub and tried to look in the mirror, but I couldn't see. All I could think about was the potential punishment I was going to endure because her white sheets had blood on them. I tried hiding it and throwing the top sheet over the bottom sheet quickly so my foster sister Patches wouldn't see it and tell on me. I was scared to death and had no clue that this was a girl thing. In those days schools had to get permission slips from our parents allowing us to see a film about menstrual cycles and it was a big, big secret amongst the kids at school. I had no friends to confide in since we were not allowed to have friends. At school, when girls got the permission slip to take home and sign, Mom would rip mine up and tell me it was for sinners and I would learn soon enough. If we didn't bring the slip back to school, we didn't watch the special movie with the other girls. We had to sit in class with the boys. I was the only girl who was not allowed to see this movie; not only did the boys look at me funny, but the girls treated me like I was an outcast and I wasn't as good or as smart as the rest of them.

In my heart I knew Mom was punishing me knowing she would sign this permission slip for Patches but not for me. Surely, I was to be scorned and humiliated just like Jesus was; surely Jesus was my Father. My childhood pain always made me think about Jesus' pain on the cross and His torture when all He wanted to do was to love and be loved, just like me. I cried for Jesus and I cried for myself. I felt I could identify with some of His pain and humiliation. Truth is—because He willingly endured that pain and humiliation—He understands us and our experiences. I didn't yet comprehend it all but I did know that Jesus died for me. Even if I wasn't put to death, I felt broken, choked, and unable to cry out for anyone to comfort me.

So the morning my bed had blood on the white sheets my foster sister, Patches, knew I was trying to hide something in my sheets. When I returned from the bathroom trying to figure out where the blood was coming from, she told me I was in big trouble and that Mom was going to kill me. I believed her and started crying and trying to wash the blood out with a cloth. Mom heard the commotion and stood in our bedroom doorway looking stern, mad, and unforgiving. She told me to get a clean sheet and meet her in the bathroom. Oh, no! Please, not the bathroom. She sat on the toilet seat with open large diaper pins in her mouth and had me strip down to nothing and stand in front of her. She seemed so angry as she pulled the white sheet from my hands and she tore the sheet in strips; long, hard, and loud tares. She told me I would never forget this day for the rest of my life.

I knew I was going to die but I could not figure out what she was going to do with those sheets and the big diaper pins. I really had no idea; perhaps she was going to hang me after she tied me up or puncture me with the pins. After all, she had tied my brothers up, why not me? I had ironed all those sheets, every pillowcase, each tablecloth, and anything else that shouldn't have wrinkles. After Mom had torn the sheet to pieces, she pinned one piece around my waist, then the other sheet pieces she had me stand with my legs apart and she put one of those strips between my legs and pinned it to the cloth that was around my waist. If I bled on it, I had to put another clean sheet strip between my legs and then in the evenings, I would have to wash those bloody rags and hang them outside on the clothesline. It wasn't bad enough I was a bed wetter but now I was a bleeder. What was wrong with me? Did Jesus bleed, too? He did, but it was on the cross and he was bleeding because of wounds on his body. He willingly shed his blood for you and me. When they mocked Him, He had the power to come down off that cross but He chose to stay, to cover the penalty for our sins.

I did not have any friends to share this with. I was sure I was the only girl in the house who had such a problem. Why me? Later, I realized that there were boxes of pads in the bathroom that were for such a time as this, but that wasn't until after I had moved out of Mrs. H's house. I didn't even realize until I was pregnant why I bled each month, or why I even had a belly button. It wasn't until I gave birth to my first child at nineteen that I realized the child didn't pop out of the belly button. Honestly the first time a man put his tongue in my mouth, I knew for sure I was going to be pregnant. Had I known that the tongue wasn't the culprit, I would have never ever rushed this young man to the altar. I thought his tongue did that and I was determined to have a healthy life, and being married in this condition was the only honorable thing, right? My dad got my mother pregnant at the age of fifteen, so this man with his nasty tongue would have to marry me, too. Of course once we were married, this young man showed me how it was really done and the rest is history—history which could have unfolded another direction if I had received proper education about menstrual cycles and pregnancies, but those issues were taboo while I lived with the H's.

Other unique tortures were perpetrated on my brothers while living with Mrs. H. She seemed to particularly enjoy pouring liquid heat all over my brother Chief's body and then making him stand in the sunshine to enhance the pain. For those of you who don't know what liquid heat is, let me explain. In our days it was almost like a liquid version of Icy Hot but without the cooling ice side.

There was also Mrs. H's stepson, Carrot Top, who loved to tease and torture Little Leroy and Chief too. Carrot Top was in his early teen years and I guess teenage boys are supposed to tease but Carrot Top was just plain mean. I never saw laughter come from my two brothers while Carrot Top was picking on them. Carrot Top liked to rub my brothers' noses under his armpits and lock them outside in the dark, knowing they were afraid of the dark. One time he led them downstairs into an unlit cold basement and shut the door and locked them in while laughing as he heard them crying out in anguish. He was definitely a brutish teenager. He may have had a beautiful head of Carrot Top hair, but he was cruel, cunning, and compassionless. He was good at acting innocent and pointing blame at my little brothers and he never got punished, neither did my foster sister. It seemed that those two were the privileged children. I was certain it was because they were not foster children.

My foster sister was the princess. She even looked the part with her golden blonde hair, petite body, new clothes, and shoes. She took ballet and tap dance classes and piano lessons. She never had to rub Mom's feet. She didn't have to bow down and pray at Mom's feet. She didn't get the belt whippings for anything and I know that when she was sick she didn't have to eat her puke. She traveled to Disneyland and San Francisco with relatives but not us. Whenever we were fortunate enough to go to the San Joaquin Lake, she didn't have to do any work or chores at the lake before she got to dive into the water. However, my brothers and I had to snap a large brown bag of green beans before we got to dive in. My sister's bathing suit was new and fit her perfectly, not like mine. My bathing suit was always big, where the crotch hung near my knees and its bust was as large as my shoulders, when I had no bust at all. My brothers wore cutoff jeans, which I would have gladly worn. But it seemed Mom intentionally wanted to humiliate me so that the other children would laugh and make fun of me. I tried to run into the water before anyone could see my bathing suit and tried to stay in the deep end so they couldn't see it, just my head. Eventually I had to come out and face the humiliation.

Patches got to take mini vacations during school breaks while my brothers and I held down the fort. In other words, we never had a single vacation, nor did we deserve it, but still it was hurtful to experience the inequity as children. We were to learn how to make a living and if all the chores were done perfectly, perhaps we could go outside and pretend we had toys. Mom used to say, "Make do with what you've got." So if we wanted to play store, we dug through the garbage can and pulled out empty cans and lids pretending we had a grocery story. We made mud pies, decorated them with chinaberries or leaves, and placed them in the shortening can lids. My brothers carried wood and made a frame for our store. No sooner than we got set up and were having a good time, Mom would see us and call us in for a new chore. It was as though she couldn't stand to see us taking pleasure in anything. It seemed to make her angry. She would tell us we better clean that mess (our pretend store) outside, pronto.

Patches had paper dolls, real paper dolls. I, on the other hand, had to make mine from Sears magazines. I would pretend to love my paper dolls as much as she loved her real paper dolls. When she got new clothes for school, we got new secondhand clothes but we always got new underwear and socks since they made for good Christmas and birthday gifts. Yet, Patches got real toys, games, ballerina clothes, special things for her hair, and a jewelry box with a little ballerina dancing inside. I remember she got the cutest little china tea set; it was made of glass and small enough for a two-year-old's fingers. I was envious and really wanted a set for myself. I suppose I was jealous and couldn't understand the injustice of underprivileged children not being treated as fair as any other children. All children deserve to be treated with love and respect, but not Little Leroy, Chief, or me. Obviously there was something wrong with us and we were different.

I remember one Christmas our real mother sent a Christmas box for my brothers and me; it was the only time she had ever sent us Christmas gifts. She even visited us once; she lived 36 miles away in Dos Palos, the same town where my father lived with his second wife. But back to the Christmas box our real mom sent. Our gift had new clothes and toys and I especially remember a beautiful hand muff. It was pure white, with a kitten head on it and both my little hands fit perfectly into it. Chief, Little Leroy, and I sat down in the kitchen watching Mrs. H open our gifts and let us look at them but not touch them or try them on. However, she let me hold the kitten hand muff. Then she put everything back into the big box and told us that she wouldn't let us have them because our mother was trying to buy our love and it was too late for that. She informed us that she would give our gifts to children who could use them. I still can't comprehend how someone could be so cruel and callous. Mrs. H seemed intent on breaking our hearts. Although I knew I was to be treated like my Father in heaven, didn't Jesus get to keep the gifts the Wise Men brought him when He was born? I didn't understand why Mrs H would give our one and only Christmas gifts to children who deserve them more than the three of us. There was obviously something wrong with her as she apparently derived pleasure from hurting us emotionally and mentally as well as physically. I can understand why my birth mother never bought us any more gifts after that occasion. Our real mom came to visit after Christmas and of course asked how we liked our gifts. We were not allowed to tell her what Mrs. H had done with them but somehow she found out. Mrs. H wouldn't allow our mother to gloat over us and a hug when she got there and hug when she left was all we were allowed. I know my heart wanted to cry, cling, beg, and tell her we would be real, real good if she would please take us out of this horrible home! However, it was ingrained in us that children were to be seen and not heard. Besides, we knew our foster mom watched our every move and we were just a beating away if we disobeyed. We were three little stones not allowed to love our mommie back. How sad my mommie must have felt. She also must have felt guilty to some degree at the very least that she had only come to visit us twice in seven year. Like I said, she and my dad only lived 36 miles away. It's as if they had thrown away their family like garbage. We were their rejects and they just moved on to other wives, husbands, and had more kids.

Do I think abortion in this circumstance would have been better for us? Heck, no! Life is a challenge for all of us, some more than others. Jesus didn't have it easy either, and I am His daughter. I do know that if I hadn't received the nun/angel's words at my Holy Communion, I wouldn't have been able to endure the pain and suffering. God gave me those words to cling to!

Our church announced there would be a bus trip to see Rev. Billy Graham in Fresno, California. I had seen him on television because we were allowed to watch some TV, news, and church stuff only. He was well known for delivering a healing message of love to broken and hurting folks. I heard him say that our Father wouldn't judge or condemn us as He came to deliver us and that this Father would never leave me or forsake me. This Father loved and wanted us orphan children! I really wanted to meet Billy Graham, this man of God! The opportunity came where a school bus from one of our churches took a group to a Billy Graham Crusade in Fresno. I was blessed to go—not my brothers this time—just me.

I was at an awkward age. What's worse I was considered ugly, fat, and wore secondhand clothes that were too big so I could grow into them and save money in the long run. I wore boys' shoes because Mom said that they lasted longer. My head was shaved in the back and the rest of my hair was two inches long and I had to use butch wax to keep it pulled away from my face. This is just a brief description of what I looked like so you can have a better understanding of why the other children on the bus wouldn't sit next to me. At that time in my life, I thought that even I wouldn't have sat with me in such a condition. They crowded each other on a seat rather than sit comfortably with me. Although this was a Christian retreat, there were not any nice kids on this bus. I sat alone. I remember sitting next to the window and placing my face on the window. It was cold and I could see my reflection. I prayed and begged God, "Father, would you please give me a family who loves me and wants me? Please, Jesus. Amen."

When we arrived at the Billy Graham Crusade, I tried to be the first person off the bus so I could be the first to be touched by Billy. I also wanted to avoid the smears and verbal abuse the kids would throw at me as they passed my seat. I was first to dash off the bus, but I had to wait for everyone to unload and march into the Crusade together. Luckily the bus driver and another adult led us. I was next to them and felt assured that no one would do the pig calls or make fun of me as long as I stood next to the adults. Yet, how could the adults ignore my outward condition? Who needed to be saved more than me? I knew if I could hear the message Billy Graham preached I would be saved! In my childlike innocence, I thought Billy Graham could open a window from heaven so Jesus could see me more clearly!

I forgot about the prayer I prayed that night on the school bus until years later when I was attending another Billy Graham Crusade in Pasadena, California. I was sitting on bleachers behind my son, Strongwind; daughter-in-law, Veronica; and grandsons. While we were singing, the Lord reminded me of the prayer on the school bus. Just like I asked so many years ago, here I was with a family who loved me and wanted me. It didn't happen when I wanted it to happen, but it meant so much more to me that night under the stars when Jesus reminded me of that prayer and His answer. Of course I cried as I hugged my grandsons and kissed my son and daughter-in-law. A precious moment in my hell as a teenager was answered many years later....He is faithful!

I reached an age where I started to think that maybe now I was normal; I just didn't have a normal family. That didn't even sound logical! How could I be normal if I came from an abnormal family? I learned how to make myself look like the other kids. I rolled up my skirts from below my knees to above my knees, tied my blouse in front making me look slimmer, I snuck my Sunday shoes under my armpits, and stole Mom's sample lipsticks she got from Avon. I lined my eyes with pencil or crayons. I learned how to tease my hair and I had to do all this before the school bus picked us up. Yes, my brothers and I learned how to beat Mrs. H's attempt to make us look pitiful to the world. She had the idea that if we wore worldly clothes and shoes and wore the colors black and red that we would turn into our parents. We could not listen to rock music or any music other than school or church music. Rock music was of the devil himself. So my brothers and I got clever and the three little rascals turned into three teenage rascals. You could beat us and torture us, but you couldn't break us—not completely. We made it to junior high school and those kids were vicious. Kids don't hold their tongues. Pushing you into lockers or tripping you was the normal way to treat nerds like us.

My life finally began to have music when I started sneaking around. I felt like I could be a star for a moment. People looked at me in a good way. I felt special. I was shy and innocent. The other kids suddenly wanted me around now that I looked pretty. One day that all changed. Mrs. H sent me to school on the bus but she forgot to tell me that I had a dentist appointment. She showed up at school later that day to pick me up. When my teacher got a phone call from the school office, she told me to get my books together because my mother was on her way to pick me up. I stood up beside my desk, the classroom door opened, and there stood Mrs. H. She hardly recognized me. I wasn't wearing the boy's brown oxford shoes, my skirt wasn't covering my calves, the blouse wasn't tucked in, and the sweater she had me wear to hide my growing boobs was nowhere to be found. Plus I had lipstick on and my eyes had makeup. My heart was pounding so fast that I thought I was going to faint and I began to sweat profusely. Surely, this was the day I would witness a new torture and maybe even finally end up dead. She didn't say a word to me, but she couldn't wait to grab my ears with her fingernails. I deserved it. I was cunning, deceitful, and deserved whatever torture she came up with and I needed to bear my cross just like Jesus did. He was probably ashamed of me, too. Was He?

Mrs. H drove me to the railroad tracks and told me to get out and stand on the tracks because a train hitting me would be better than what I was going to get at home. Again I was scared to death and really at that time of my life I wanted to die anyway. I was a bad girl, probably would turn out to be like my tramp mother. Why did every other kid get to have a glorious life and have fun times? Why were my brothers and I punished daily? Why us? I stared at the railroad tracks and started to get out of the car. Just then, she dug her nails into my arm and told me we had an appointment and I wasn't going to make her look bad by breaking that appointment. I did what I was told and every moment I grew more wary of what torture was going to be inflicted on me. My stomach was turning, my neck and brows were dripping with sweat. Maybe she would burn me again. Maybe this time she would put my hand or face over the flames of the stove. Maybe she would take me back to school and let the children see my back and legs with all the old and new wounds from the strap. Or perhaps she would make me sleep on the railroad tracks until a train ran me over. Perhaps she and Dad would put me in a gunnysack, hit me over the head with a board, then hide my body in the river. Maybe they would hack off my head like they did to the chickens. I cried the entire time I was in the dentist office, all the while he tried to calm my nerves. He thought that I was afraid of him and his dentistry. I wasn't allowed to talk more than a "Yes, sir" or "No, sir." That's all children were allowed to say. I was scared to death and the moments leading to our arrival at home were pure anguish. After we left the dentist's office, she wanted me to parade in front of Dad so he could see what a shameful sight I was.

When we got home I had to sit at the kitchen table, hands folded in my lap as always, and told to wait. Who knew what Mrs. H was going to come up with? Whatever it was, I deserved it. Look at me. I looked like a whore, yet before she showed up at school I had felt good about myself. I made myself sick and I knew when I threw up I was going to have to ingest it because I was in the kitchen and no one throws up in her kitchen. I threw up, but I didn't have to ingest it this time. I had to clean it up, then march to the bathroom and wait some more. She sure knew how to torture a kid; I think waiting was the worst. The waiting was finally over. I got my butt whipped to the point of not being able to sit. It was dreadful. I had painful leather strap marks upon strap marks, old wounds opened up and new wounds upon areas that never had a chance to heal, but I deserved each lashing; unlike Jesus, who didn't deserve a single strike. All I could say was, "I'm sorry, Mommy, I won't do it again … I'm sorry, Mommy. I won't do it again."

My brothers were in middle school and they heard my mom had come to school to pick me up. Their little bodies started trembling because they knew I had been caught. They knew they would be tortured because they went along with my behavior. I didn't give them up and I lied to protect them, but they got their butts whipped anyway, although not as bad as I did. She didn't have time. She needed to make dinner and Dad was due home any minute. I was still sitting in the kitchen with my earlier garb, but now my makeup was washed away with tears and my rolled up skirt was below my knees again.

Dad didn't pay any attention to me. He seemed to ignore his wife when he was home. Home was hers to control; outdoors was his to control. So I only had to worry about tomorrow when I returned to school looking my ugly self. Luckily first period was PE so I thought that maybe I could wear my gym sweats and tennis shoes. Maybe? No such luck. Our PE teacher told us to dress out in our shorts since it was a beautiful day outside and we would run laps first. I couldn't put my shorts on. I put my sweats on because I didn't want the kids to see the lashes on my thighs because they would know I was a bad girl. My teacher told me to go back to the locker room and put on the proper gear or she would give an F for the day and call my mom. She said, "Charli, you have a nice shape, so don't be ashamed of it. Put your shorts on." I started crying. I either showed her I was a bad girl or I would get an F and another whooping. She knew I was upset and waited for me at the exit door. When she saw me in shorts she gave me a pat on the head, but then I could hear her gasp as I walked away from her towards the other girls.

She noticed my legs and all the scars and wounds. She had me go back to locker room and wait. She called the school nurse and principal. *Wow, I am really in trouble now*, I thought. My brothers were also called into the office. I was told to get dressed in my regular clothes and go to the office. The school nurse examined me and my brothers. We never went back to Mr. and Mrs. H's home again. We were rescued. The school authorities wanted to know why we never told anyone what was happening to us. Really, who could we tell? The police and social services were the ones who took us to their choice of homes and dropped us off all those years ago. Also, we were taught that children were to be seen and not heard. We were not allowed to voice anything other than "Yes, ma'am" or "No, ma'am" or "Yes, sir" or "No, sir." I knew that trying to keep three of us together in one home was a major issue when we were first placed there in 1956, seven years ago. We were a problem and who volunteers to take on problems? Not our parents, not the police, not the courts, not the school system. Everyone in authority was passing the buck and we were the buck. Now we were just teenage problems. Who wanted little—and now big—rascals?

Jesus came for people like us. He came for the brokenhearted, wounded, unwanted, and the orphans. Somehow in some way this would all turn around for His glory. Perhaps some good would come out of this and it did.

San Joaquin County took away the other children who were living with Mr. and Mrs. H and Social Services started training programs for foster parents. It wasn't enough any longer to just volunteer to be foster parents. You now had to be trained. That was a good thing. Now children didn't have to be hurt like we were. Mandatory reporting laws to protect children from abuse were beginning to spread across the country at that time. People in occupations such as doctors, nurses, and teachers who had contact with children, were required to report any suspected child abuse or neglect to authorities.

Perhaps we paved the way so others would have it easier. Don't you think children who have to go to foster care are already wounded? They don't need to be saddened by yet another hand! This new journey was about to begin and separation of the three of us was inevitable. No foster home wanted three teenagers and the question now was "which one of us was to be separated?" I consider this a precious moment. When hope is given, it's a precious moment! My brothers needed each other. Prying them apart would have been like separating Siamese twins. A simple solution was for me to go it alone. Plenty of foster care homes wanted a teenage girl who had never been in trouble and who could cook, sew, clean, and babysit; plus, I could probably win awards as a foot massager—after all, I had nightly practice for seven years.

LIFE AFTER FOSTER CARE

"The heavens declare the glory of God; the skies proclaim the work of His hands."

PSALM 19:1 NIV

S ocial Services found my dad, Marian, and he volunteered to take my brothers. My brothers were ecstatic to be placed with our dad in Dos Palos. My mother wanted me but I didn't want my mother, because I knew she hadn't changed and I didn't want to be associated with her bar friends. I thought that her male friends would look at me like a piece of meat and I did not want any part of that lifestyle. But I didn't have a choice and had to go with her to Dos Palos.

By that time, my mother had another daughter and two more sons and I was at the perfect age to be their babysitter. I wasn't with her a whole week when Friday night came around and she was getting ready for the bar scene. There was plenty of booze in the house but there was hardly any food. Yet the four of us needed to eat. It seems inconceivable that people's priorities and consciences allow them to purchase cigarettes, booze, and soda to go with the rum and whiskey but not have enough money for milk, bread, and other food to support their children. From my point of view, they were selfish folks who had zero regard for their children; and here I was again with the same mother who had those very priorities and lack of conscience. She had the same old habits but she had three new children to neglect. I had to stay positive. My brothers Chief and Little Leroy lived just a few blocks from me with my dad, so maybe I could see them once in a while.

We lived downtown, which was walking distance to local bars where my mother did her drinking and picked up her customers. This time of the year, her customers were duck hunters. When the duck hunters were not around, it was the field workers. The field workers spoke Spanish and so did my mother. Since the workers were usually far from their families, they seemed to really enjoy the attention of my beautiful mother. She took delight in their adulation and they took pleasure in her company.

I, on the other hand, was getting prepared to run away the first chance I could if I thought my body was going to be used or violated. I had been watching a TV show that gave me the idea of using a long stick with a handkerchief tied to the end of it with my valuables in it. It looked easy to put together. All I had to do was find a stick which fit over my shoulder and a scarf to wrap up my few belongings and I was ready. I had it all together and hidden next to the bathroom window where I planned to escape when the time came.

Once I had all my belongings packed, I turned my focus on surviving. There wasn't much to eat in the house. I found some pinto beans and tried cooking them. It was the first time I had cooked pinto beans and they turned out hard as rocks. After my mom had already been at the bar a few hours or so, my sister, Peacock, and my little brothers, Baby boy, and JR, started getting really hungry. There wasn't anything else to cook or eat except those hard pinto beans. Those beans never did get soft. I simply didn't know how Mrs. H made the best-tasting chili beans from a bag of pinto beans. I didn't realize she had to cook them all day. When my mother came home that night—which was really the next morning— with a couple of her party friends, she wanted to know what the heck was in her favorite pot. They were hard beans. My half-brothers, sister, and I wouldn't have been able to eat at all that day if I hadn't contacted my dad who just happened to work a few blocks away at a car dealership. He brought over a bag of groceries—bread, bologna, potatoes chips, and a carton of milk. He came on a little scooter. He told me that when I heard him coming down the street, I needed to meet him outside since he was still supposed to be working. As soon as I heard his motor scooter with its loud high-pitched sound, I was overcome with joy. I really missed my daddy. I couldn't wait to tell my little brothers and sister, but he told me not to tell anyone, especially my mother, that the groceries were from him or he would never hear the end of it. So it was my secret and my siblings were too young to care where their food came from. They were just hungry; they were the same age that Chief, Little Leroy, and I were when we lived with my mother. Once she started drinking, she didn't care what we ate. The only difference today; I was older and since I could help, my siblings might not have to be raised in foster homes. The options; either they would go hungry and continue to be neglected by their own mother or they might live in a foster home where they would have had a bed of their own and three square meals on the table but possibly be abused. Is that fair for a teenager to have to make this choice for her siblings? At this time of my life, I thought they were better off with my mother because they were small and they were not being beaten like my brothers and I had experienced.

All I knew was that I was not going to become my mother. I was not going to have men look at me as if I were just a body to be used and I was not going to become a meal ticket for my mother to abuse. I was determined to run away the first chance I got. As the bar closed at 2:00 AM, I could hear my mother and her friends and lovers come in loud, laughing, and calling my name. "Charli! Get in here. I know you're awake. I want you to meet my friends." When she was drunk she was mean, vicious, and you did what she told you or she may break a bottle of booze on you. Whether the bottle was full or not, she didn't care. Man or woman, she didn't care. So I got up and rubbed my eyes like I was waking up, and I took my clothes to the bathroom to get dressed and pretend like I was getting ready to meet her friends.

The time had come. Instead of going in to meet the friends, as soon as I was dressed, I slipped out the bathroom window and ran to my dad's house since he didn't live too far away from my mother's. His house was dark and I didn't want to wake up his new wife and kids so I wedged myself in his alley between his garbage cans. I figured I could stay there until he got up for work. I wasn't there even an hour and I saw his lights come on and a police car met him in the alley where I was hiding. Oh great, I was sure I was going to be arrested because I ran away and my dad knew it. I was curled in a little ball as I listened to my dad and his friend, the cop. Everyone knew my dad in Dos Palos. He was a popular man who now sold cars for the best dealership in town. He was also known for his expertise with automobiles—he used to fix up motorcycles and Model T's. The people in the town had a lot of respect for him. They gave him the inside scoop on what was going on with his first wife and daughter. They let him know that I ran away and the authorities were looking for me. I heard him tell the cop there was no way he could take me, because his new wife was just getting used to having two stepsons which caused their family to grow from three to five and they didn't have a big enough house—impossible.

I heard my dad crying to this cop and telling him how he failed my brothers once and he didn't want to do it again. He hadn't spent a single minute with my brothers in the past seven years and now he could, but didn't know how to help his daughter. He knew it wasn't good for me to live with my mom because the town knew who she was and what she did for a living. It would only be a matter of time before I was forced to be the same kind of woman she was. No one seemed to realize that I had been beaten every day for seven years so I wouldn't grow up to be like my mother. There was no way I would end up like her! Just living with this mother was hell-hell on earth!

No, I'd rather run away and get sent to jail or something and take my chances there. But that night I decided I couldn't bother my father because I might rock the boat for my brothers. I headed to San Jose where my aunt D lived, and hoped that maybe she could take me in. I made it as far as the little country town airport field and cut across it to reach

Pacheco Pass highway. While in the field, spotlights were being pointed in my direction so I lay down on my back facing the sky and cried my heart out, "Why me, Lord? Why me? Do you see me? Do you care? Why can't I have a home, too? You did. You had a mom and dad who loved you and took care of you. Can you just tell me, somehow, that you care? Please God, please!"

Immediately after I cried that prayer and begged God to give me a sign, as I lay on that empty freshly plowed field, the sky filled up with shooting stars. In Job 37:5 (NLT) it says, *"God's voice is glorious in the thunder. We can't even imagine the greatness of his power."* If His children can hear Him in the thunder, why not shooting stars? I don't care what people think when I tell them what Jesus showed me, I know what I experienced! The sky was filled with falling stars and I knew God was telling me that He heard me. He sees me and He cares. That is what I call a precious moment in hell.

I continued to cry, but this time because I knew He heard me and that He was my Father who would never leave me or forsake me like everyone else had. After the star show was over, I knew I had to do the right thing and turn myself in or make it to a local church. In those days, I thought the church doors were always open, but apparently not that night. So when I couldn't get into the church for shelter, I made it to the police station and turned myself in and told them I would run away again if they made me go back to my mother's. While waiting to hear what they were going to do with me, I remembered a song I used to hear while attending various churches: "His eye is on the sparrow, and I know He watches me" written in 1905 by lyricist Civilla D Martin, composer Charles H Gabriel. I knew who my Father was, I just needed to be reminded. It seemed that the more challenging my life got, the more I needed to call on Jesus. When I was younger, it seemed that the only right time to talk to Jesus was at church or on my knees bent at Mrs. H's recliner or just before a punishment. As I got older, I realized that I could talk to Him constantly and have Him go before me; before being afflicted.

The sheriff's deputies were kind to me and understood my

circumstances, because in a small town like Dos Palos, everyone knew each other's business and my mother had been arrested many times. Two of the officers brought out two hardcover files which looked like they were four to eight inches thick. They told me it was my mother's police history and I had no hesitation in believing it was the truth. They asked if I was hungry. I loved that every time I was in a place with authority figures, they would ask if I was hungry. I was always hungry. They told me that it would be hard to find a foster home or receiving home over the weekend. They asked me if I would like to spend the rest of the weekend with a deputy's family who was good friends with my dad. Of course! I said, "Yes, sir."

Over the next couple of days I was questioned about my past. The people hearing it had a hard time swallowing: they were very uncomfortable hearing my story. I could tell because of how they fidgeted and smoked more than normal. As I observed them I thought, "Really? You already have a cigarette in your mouth and you're going to light another one?" The police and their friends could hardly believe what had taken place in my brothers' and my foster home. They wanted so much to comfort me and have me trust them. It was true that the past couldn't be fixed, but to give my brothers a future with their daddy, this was a precious moment.

Even though I was going to be taken to jail on Monday, not as a punishment, but to provide a bed and place to sleep until a good foster home could be arranged. That was a precious moment in my mind. The kind police family was going to talk to my dad just in case he could make room for me. That Monday I spent the day with my dad, my brothers, his new wife and their three daughters. It was bliss, and my dad was so delighted that he started dancing to Chubby Checker doing a dance called the Twist, he had it on TV and wanted us to watch him and dance with him. I tried but had never seen anyone dance before and watching my daddy was the treat of my life. Then it was bedtime and my dad tucked us into bed on his porch. The four of us cried happy tears. I can't remember falling asleep, but I remember my daddy tucking me in for the first time and I mused, "I sure could get use to this…." Thank you, Jesus, for another precious moment.

The following morning, my dad went to work and I tried to help my stepmother Natalie in the kitchen. However, she seemed preoccupied with her daughters and didn't want my help. I sensed she didn't like me. She probably thought I was like my mother as most people would. Here I was dropped off by the police in front of her home. What did the neighbors think? How could I expect that she knew me, we had never spoken. She only knew what my daddy told her. I stayed in the porch area so I would not get in anyone's way. I do recall my brothers and I washed the family car in the front yard. I wore a pair of shorts which attracted whistles and slowed traffic in front of my dad's home on the corner of the main street. It was warm outside and I drew attention with my wet clothes. It wasn't purposeful on my part and I innocently didn't think twice about the slowed traffic. My brothers and I wanted to please my dad and our stepmother. Since she didn't want our help indoors, perhaps we could do something good outdoors. Indeed, that was our intention.

When Dad got home from work, I could hear Natalie and Dad talking with voices raised and their body language wasn't good either. When you are raised to be seen and not heard, you become intuitive to your surroundings and I knew they were arguing about me. I didn't realize it was about the three of us until, my dad came out to the porch and said he needed some advice. Advice from his children? He proceeded, "Here it is *Mi hija*, Chief, Little Leroy … my wife can't take care of the three of you and I have to make a choice today to keep you three and leave her and my three daughters; or let you go back to foster care and keep my wife and daughters. I don't know what to do. Please help me!" This 6'5" man bent over our bed, seeming absolutely helpless as he held his head in his hands and cried his heart out. He left the room briefly which gave me a chance to talk to my brothers alone. My brothers were now thirteen and fourteen; I was fifteen. We just spent seven years in an awful home and these three little girls hadn't had to experience such a travesty. I told my brothers, "Pretty soon we will be eighteen and we can leave the foster homes. How can we let these three little girls possibly live in a foster home and also have their mother leave our daddy?" We had to go back to foster homes. We were shattered once again, not from a belt whipping but from a heartbreak. We were sobbing, clinging, crying, and holding on to each other while snot and tears drenched our clothes. We told our daddy we would go back to foster homes so he could keep his new family since we had already spent most of our childhood away from our parents. Why punish these little girls?

Luckily at the last minute my dad arranged for his brother Franklin to take my brothers. I slept at the juvenile hall for nearly six weeks. Each of these moments of hell seemed to draw me to a song I learned in Sunday school. I would hear a melody just as I had on the night I lay in that field looking up at the sky and witnessed the spectacular shooting stars show. This time the melody playing in my head was, "I come to the garden alone...while the dew is still on the roses...and a voice I hear fell upon my ears, the Son of God discloses. And He walks with me, and He talks with me, and He tells me I am His own. And the voice I hear falling on my ears...." I knew He was talking to me and wooing me, "everything was going to be all right." The song "Jesus loves me—this I know" and "The Old Rugged Cross" always reminds me of His love for people like me and every time I hear those songs or sing them, it lifts my spirit and causes joy and tears and peace. On the day my brothers and I were separated, I heard the song, "I serve a Risen Savior. He is in the world today. I know that He is living, no matter what men may say." I don't understand why I heard that song that day, but I sang it and knew He was lifting my spirit up to Him. In the world I was as low as I could be—no home, no parents, no family, and unaware of where my tomorrows would take me. But I serve a Savior who is in the world today!

More Hard Lessons

"The LORD corrects those he loves, as parents correct a child of whom they are proud."

PROVERBS 3:12 GW

When my stepmother decided we were not welcomed and dad gave us the ultimatum, my brothers and I were separated for the rest of our youth. They went one way and I another. My first big stop was juvenile hall. Trust me, when I walked into juvenile hall, I didn't look like the rest of the juveniles locked up. I looked like a goody two shoes girl. I was extremely naive and could understand why the officers kept me as far from the convicted juveniles as possible. But that only made me a target for icy-cold stares from the juvenile delinquents. Sometimes when I looked at these girls, they would slide their finger across their neck in a threatening manner. Other times they would flip the familiar hand gesture, the middle finger. I was so naïve I didn't even know what that gesture meant but I could tell it clearly wasn't good because there was malice in their eyes. My naivety showed so that everyone, the juvenile delinquents and staff included, knew I was a novice in this new world of hell that was thrust upon me, this prison called juvenile hall. Surely I was one of God's kids, since Jesus and His disciples had also been imprisoned. I am His daughter and was being treated just like Jesus was treated. He never had a permanent place to lay His head, traveling from one location to another, not knowing from day to day where He would end up, just like me.

After the six weeks in juvenile hall, I then moved from foster home to foster home over the next three years: homes for the next three years: two fabulous homes and two not so good. I could tell when I was wanted; some families truly attempted to improve my world. I could also tell when families only wanted to use me; as a babysitter or for a government check, etc. I was so embarrassed by one of the families that when I was enrolled in school, I assumed an alias for several reasons: first, I didn't want kids to think these folks were related to me and I wanted the small community to feel sorry for me instead of knowing my real background. I quickly made up a lie that both of my parents were beheaded in a car accident. The second part of the lie; I needed a temporary place to stay and this was the only home available at the time.

Total lies, but the sympathy poured in. Not only did everyone feel sorry that I had to live with this embarrassing family, but I had lost both parents in an awful car accident. I won their sympathy for a few days until my social worker came to the school to see how I was doing and couldn't locate me. According to the school's records, the only new girl in school was named Charlene, not Charli, and the last name was incorrect too. I can't even remember what last name I used, but I learned a lesson that day. I was called to the school office and immediately recognized the social worker. It was like seeing Mrs. H all over again the day she picked me up for my dentist appointment. My stomach was turning, I was sweating around my brow, and I was completely speechless. I couldn't even think of how to swallow. I had been caught and my guilt took over. Of course I knew I had done wrong, but I had to survive and didn't think I would get punished for this little white lie. But the Lord doesn't like lying even though He is gracious. He allowed my sins to be found out. No fibbers on His ship!

Mrs. Shultz, my social worker, was as tall as Mrs. H and just her size—large. She put her arm around my shoulders and said, "You are leaving school for the rest of the day, Charlene!" Once we were in her car, she said we were going to my father's office in Dos Palos so I could tell him the story about his car accident, losing his head and all. Oh my goodness, why? I hadn't seen my dad for a few months and now I had to face him when I didn't even know if I liked him or loved him, but for sure I didn't trust him. Why put more shame on me? What would that accomplish, what was she thinking? We entered the Ford dealership and waited for him to meet and greet his client. He could talk anyone into driving away with an automobile. When he saw the woman, my social worker, he shook her hand. As soon as he took her hand, he saw me and then realized I was with her. He didn't hug me. He just took a seat behind his desk folded his hands and asked, "What can I do for you?" I was deeply hurt as I thought, "Really, not even a hug?" He was probably thinking I was a new problem for him or child support might be the issue. I don't know what he thought, but I was there to tell him my lie.

She made me stand up and tell him, and I told him like I had no shame, because as far as I was concerned, he and my birth mother were dead. I was angry. My brothers and I had been in a vicious home for seven years. They both lived 36 miles from that foster home. My father never came to visit us—not Christmas or birthdays. If he didn't have the courage to visit, how about sending a gift on Christmas or our birthdays? I still can't imagine why a parent wouldn't want to please their child at least once or twice a year. Do you know anyone like that? I was devastated! My dad shook his head from left to right and shed a tear. Good! Happy, as he was known, was speechless. At this stage of my life, all I had learned to do was to cry and say, "I'm sorry, Dad. I am sorry, Mom. I won't do it again." That was my sentence every morning when my brothers and I were whipped. "I am sorry, Mom. I won't do it again." I just leaned on the social worker and told her I was sorry too, and I wouldn't lie anymore. After we left she dropped me back at the school's office. I had to correct my name on the school records. It was time for me to grow up and handle my business. However, she didn't make me tell the truth about the car accident and the chopped off heads; that was between us.

She understood, and I wouldn't be in this school much longer anyway. I sometimes have to explain to my children why I move around so much and I tell them that the Lord conditioned my life for movement. A young mother who couldn't handle her family had caused my brothers and me to live in multiple receiving homes, later foster homes. Constant uprooting! It basically prepared me to live in a glass of Holy Spirit realm. I go with His flow which is always rich and adventurous!

Next, I was placed with another family who had eight daughters ranging in age from one to eight years old. Each daughter had an eye disease or deformity, either they were missing an eye socket or one eye was larger than the other. It was sad. They lived on a ranch in San Joaquin which meant they didn't have to live under the scorning eyes of the world. The house was up a dirt lane about two miles off the main road. I was driven to the bus stop each morning. I didn't last long there because I was missing too much school—babysitting the daughters as this mother had her hands full getting these little ones to the doctors. I felt sorry for her. Her life was full of chores and children but at least she was the best mother she could be. She didn't abandon her family even when her eight daughters were broken. I would have understood if she had. They were all broken yet their mommy and daddy stuck with them. My brothers and I were pretty much perfect physically but our parents abandoned us. Mrs. W needed me and each one of her daughters loved being in my arms or hanging on to me. I felt loved and appreciated. It was nice to feel someone wanted me. At least, that is what I thought at the time. I didn't realize I was being used and that not going to school wasn't in my best interest. I was a "do-gooder" and didn't know it. I learned a few things from living with Mrs. W. I learned how to cook, clean, and be gentle to broken children. Like my brothers, I just assumed the position wherever I was placed. I didn't have a choice now, did I? In actuality, wherever we are placed, we may not be able to control what others do, but we always have the choice of how to respond.

One of the best foster homes I lived in had a young man who was eighteen years old and a freshman in college. I was sixteen. He was shy and quiet. He had a little pad in the backyard where he and his friends would gather several times a week and on weekends. He never talked to me, nor I to him. After all, this was his home and I never knew if I was wanted or if someone was just trying to do a good deed for the community by taking in a foster child. His name was Luis and he had some good-looking friends. He was good looking too, but who was I to think he would look at me? I had nothing, no education, no parents, a history with a whore mother and a father who abandoned his kids. What kind of stock was I made out of? So how dare I think I was anything other than another mouth to feed or that he thought anything of me other than taking his parents' attention away from him. I was no one to be respected. I was nothing. I had low self-esteem. Today I don't consider any of those thoughts because I know who I am—I am a daughter of the King! But when I was sixteen, it was extremely hard to think about things in that way.

One day while I was washing the dishes, he came into the kitchen and tried to talk to me. I know now that he was trying to make me feel accepted, but as a kid who was taught to be seen and not heard, I was clueless on how to respond except to bow my head, giggle, and feel a sheet of warmth run over me. I dropped a glass and broke it. I was frantic. He tried to help me clean it up and calm my nerves. I didn't know how my new mom and dad would react to this mistake and if I would be in trouble, but he assured me it was his fault and not to worry. I couldn't get to my bedroom fast enough.

I had the most amazing bedroom in the world in this foster home! It was almost as large as some of the houses I lived in when I lived with my real mother. It had a TV, a closet filled with clothes, and shoes and purses for me, a large mirror in which I could see my whole reflection. We had a front door which led to a foyer which was so big I could dance in it. I felt so little compared to the size of this mansion and now I knew a college student too! I felt like I had the most amazing life! Luis had college friends over who would look at me and smile, then look at Luis like he was lucky to have such a good-looking foster sister. Then I met the kids next door, a pair of sisters and their brother. The girl, Cathy, was just about the same age as me and Shelly, her sister, was just a little bit older. They were from Wichita, Kansas, and they were the nicest girls I had ever met. Finally I had friends and a nice neighborhood, a cool brother, and parents from the right side of town.

In San Joaquin, there was the bad side of town and a great side of town. I lived next door to a beauty queen and we lived on the north side of Bear Creek, which was the opposite side of town from where my mother was raising us when we got picked up. I had the chance of a lifetime to live a normal life and I blew it, but not before Luis and I kissed. It wasn't a nose-to-nose kiss; it was more like he held me with my back pressed up against his chest and he kissed me on the sides of my forehead, but that kiss made me feel weak and excited, scared, clueless and sinful. I didn't think it was okay and it certainly wasn't something that I would share with Luis's mom or dad but I shared it with Cathy and Shelly. They wanted to know all about it and I trusted them enough to tell them every detail. We became best friends. The other college boys wanted to meet Cathy and Shelly. I didn't think my new mom and dad would like the new friends of mine if they thought we were up to shenanigans. So I learned quickly to interject ideas into conversations and allow others to run with those thoughts. It's amazing what a little team of young people can whip up in a few minutes.

They wanted to mix some Kool-Aid with the wine that was in the refrigerator! That was totally foreign to my thought pattern and besides, look at my mother who drank something like that. When she started to drink, the next thing you knew she was taking her clothes off and having sex, right? What else does that lead to? But they wanted to drink so we could loosen up and have a good time. That wasn't my way of thinking but my new friends who had always had their real mom and dad were beginning to embrace their rebellious years. If they wanted to do those things, it must be okay. That must be how normal people live. Who was I to think otherwise? I was the girl who didn't ever get to sit in the front row. Heck, I was lucky if I was in the same building unless someone allowed me to enter their world. I was thinking, *I am accepted.* They want to do things with me and if I do the things they do perhaps I'll grow up to be like them. Today we call that peer pressure. I didn't even know what peer pressure was then. All I could think of was, "What the heck, why not try a little wine in the daily Kool-Aid? Besides, Jesus did a miracle and turned water into wine. He's my dad, He made it, so it can't be all bad." My silly thinking took me right to the refrigerator where Cathy and Shelly were lookouts, telling me how to do it and how much to mix while looking out the kitchen window where Luis and his friends were. It was the perfect time to sneak our concoction while the college boys were playing loud music out in Luis's hut. Then suddenly here he came, headed to the kitchen door. We scooted ourselves straight to my bedroom with our individual glasses and locked my door laughing, sweating, and looking at each other like we'd gotten away with something. And then ... one of us farted! That was a surprise and awful stinky, plus a total giveaway with an explosion of laughter, not very stealth. None of the three of us claimed ownership, just so much laughter that we were audible through the walls. Then someone banged on the door to shut us up. I don't know who it was but silence overcame us and we put our finger over our mouths as a way to tell each other not to say a word. My room was filled with silence except for quiet giggling. We sipped our Kool-Aid and got a little tipsy. Now we knew we could get away with making this alcoholic Kool-Aid and get the attention of the college boys. The boys were a little shy and my girlfriends from Kansas were the friendliest girls I had ever met. Their warm smiles and friendly attitudes made me want to move to Kansas. Isn't that where Dorothy from the Wizard of Oz was from? Cathy and Shelly reminded me of Dorothy because the only people from Kansas that I had met were just as kind and trusting as Dorothy. I believed they were my friends and they accepted me. What could be better than being sixteen and having great friends on the right side of town?

There was one thing I didn't like about those two girls. They smoked cigarettes on the sly. Their parents would never have approved even though they smoked as did Don, the girls' older brother. I had been taught it wasn't ladylike and knew we shouldn't be smoking at our young ages. They always had a pack of cigarettes and smoked at the railroad underpass on the way to school. I had to wait with them while they smoked. It made me cough and hurt my throat just to stand near them. They threatened to leave me alone if I didn't try it. Threatening to leave me alone sent a chill running through my body like my blood running through my veins. People had been leaving me alone for as long as I could remember. Now, unless I tried smoking my new friends would leave me too. So I tried it but didn't like it. How could I live through the thought of not being accepted or worse, outright rejected? It was paramount that I make it up to them and show them I could be cool without smoking. I knew that one day I would be able to prove to my girlfriends I was cool just like them.

That day finally came. My girlfriends and I were on our way to high school. We stopped at the small neighborhood grocery store to buy cigarettes. They showed me how they got two packs for the price of one and insisted on my participation. I was supposed to just watch and then do exactly what they did. Those were my instructions. While Cathy stood at the counter talking and mesmerizing the man behind the register with her incredibly gorgeous good looks, her sister slipped a pack of cigarettes up her long sleeve jacket. So that was how they got the second pack for free! Next was my turn! I couldn't do it. So the girls left me in the dust. I wasn't allowed to walk with them to the tunnel. If I wanted to be their friend I had to prove my loyalty by going back into the store and stealing something … anything. An added pressure, I had to do it in the amount of time it took them to finish smoking their cigarettes. They gave me one last chance to retrieve my dignity and prove my loyalty. So, I marched myself right back into that store and took a cloth hairband off a stock wheel and slipped it into my sleeve while the store clerk and I looked at each other, eye to eye. He was watching me steal but I was too embarrassed to take it out of my sleeve. As soon as I walked out the door, the store clerk told me he had called the cops. I had a twenty-dollar bill in my wallet from babysitting and offered to pay for it, but he said it was too late.

That instant that I gave into peer pressure cost me the best home I had ever had in my whole life. I wasn't allowed to return to that home, not even to pack. Where was God at this moment? He was watching me. He allowed me to be removed from the best home I ever had. My "friends" were nowhere to be found after watching me get arrested. It was probably for the best, because Luis and I were getting a little too close. Even an accidental run-in in the kitchen made my blood boil. That must have been the devil in us—you know, the one Mrs. H was always trying to beat out of me.

Later I found out that Shelly married my foster brother Luis and they had several children together. I lost, she won, and truthfully speaking they were never my true friends. They were just another lesson in life. A lesson which taught me to never steal or go along with peer pressure ever again.

Is there a precious moment in this episode?

Yes, but I wouldn't see it until I had children of my own.

After many years of being out of foster homes, I had a new life. I decided that I wanted to take my well-loved children back to Mrs. H's house. I would have the reins then. I wanted her to see that I didn't turn out like my mother and that I raised my children the way I wanted to be raised, with lots of love and care.

I took my kiddos and visited Mr. and Mrs. H a couple times a year. One day she confided in me why she was so mean to us while we were living in her home. She said that she was angry with Mr. H, her second husband. She felt he never loved her, caressed her, or complimented her. She was always angry at him and took it out on the three of us. Hurt people hurt others. Again Jesus' example guides us—*"Jesus said, 'Father, forgive them, for they do not know what they are doing'..."* (Luke 23:34 NIV)

Mrs. H also told me she had other foster children in and out of her home, but to us she had behaved differently. She had to keep her word to show she was honest and consistent with what she said. That first day we met her, she said she would do such and such and therefore she just had to. After all what type of Christian would she be if she were a liar? Perhaps a very mixed-up Christian? She was human and truthfully we all have different things we are dealing with. Christians aren't perfect, we make mistakes too. And one of our big mistakes is when we don't go to our Father for guidance. *"If any of you lacks wisdom, let him ask God, who gives generously to all without reproach, and it will be given him."* (James 1:5 ESV)

Anyway, Mrs. H was raised in a Christian home. Her father was a Methodist preacher and a missionary from the South. She was also raised during the Great Depression which didn't help us either. The Great Depression left its own scars on people. Mrs. H felt compelled to save everything like our lunch sacks and the sandwich bags and menstrual pads. It was all about cost savings yet for my brothers and me it was humiliating.

It wasn't until nearly fifty-five years later that I considered the other children who went through the H's home and experienced some of her ways. My foster sister Patches, the princess, contacted my brothers and me. She told us that as soon as we were taken from Mrs. H, she ran away from home but she could not for the life of her remember why. I was so consumed with our pain that I never considered how the other children must have been impacted when we were being tortured. Were they scared for themselves or for us? Did they feel helpless? There was no way that they could escape our cries. They surely heard our cries even though we were supposed to be quiet while we were being spanked. They had to have heard the cries of my brothers when they were locked outside in the dark. I couldn't understand how people allowed those cries to go unnoticed. Or, was everything a secret as long as it happened inside a house? Fifty-five years later, I learned that Patches was so traumatized by just witnessing the torture that was perpetrated on us that she blocked those years out of her memory. It wasn't until she was almost seventy that she started to look for us and see if we could help her to recall this part of her life. Her childhood memories were lost.

One of those memories was the time I asked Mom to button the back of my long secondhand dress which must have had ten buttons. How does one button the back of a dress without help? While the same moment I asked for help, so did Patches. She asked to have her dress zipped; Mom reached over and zipped Patches' dress but told me, "If you are the only person in the world, who would button your dress? Where there is a will there is a way!" Why was my position different from Patches, unless Patches' life was going to be one with help and mine would be one without help? It was obvious that we were being schooled differently. I knew Patches had to be aware that we were being treated disparately but I was oblivious to the notion that Patches would be feeling any pain as she wasn't being mistreated, rather she was being lavished upon. Yet, Patches was crying on the inside for our pain and she couldn't show it so she bottled it up in her little soul. How could she know how to react unless she was taught and her teacher was a cruel and wicked woman. It never occurred to me she was being damaged too.

That was a hard learned lesson seeing how one action can impact many others in many different ways. This is one of the important reasons why God tells us to *"be kind to one another, tenderhearted, forgiving one another, as God in Christ forgave you."* (Ephesians 4:32 ESV)

Life's lessons are not easy and it seems just as we finally learn one, it's off to another lesson. How does one grow unless we learn through experiences? I was learning what type of mother and person I did and did not want to be; after all, we are a product of our parenting. I had a few mothers who some might call the devil's spawn. My first two mothers didn't seem to have any of Christ in them. Or perhaps it was for Christ's sake that I had both those mothers straight from hell so that I could survive them like Daniel survived the lions' den. Surely, I have made many decisions in my life based on my experiences living with Lupe and Mrs. H.

I knew in my heart that I needed to forgive them. It was also important to forgive Luis' mom, although she'd had no forgiveness for a girl from juvenile hall. She hadn't given me a break or allowed me to explain why I stole that hairband. She just assumed I was a bad girl. Yet it was imperative that I let go of the resentment and forgive. I believe God had His hand in that separation and it was for my own good; that doesn't mean I stopped wanting Luis in my life nor did I stop looking for him to show up at any foster home I might move to. But that was not to be my future—God had other things in store.

My life was much like my true Father, moving in and out of situations where He was needed and not knowing from day to day where He would lay His head, just like me. For sure my daddy was Jesus. He came for us—the broken and shattered. He didn't judge us or hold grudges. He just loved us and wanted to be loved, just like me.

You are reading a true sinner's escapades, I'm ashamed to say you haven't heard anything yet. I started out as a little rascal: wanting to kill Mrs. H, sneaking around, telling lies, and running away. My life was a mess and I had no one to blame except myself because I chose to serve myself instead of Jesus. The problem was that I didn't know Him intimately. I just knew *about* Him but I knew with my whole heart that He knew me. He met me along the path each and every time I fell into a pit and He lifted me up. He encouraged me, He warned me, and He sometimes showed off for me, like the night the sky was full of those shooting stars.

My Father is a glory hog and I say that with the utmost respect, but who gets the glory at the end of my story? It will be Jesus, who came so that we would *"have life and have it abundantly"* (John 10:10 ESV). No, I can't say I am a millionaire if that's what you think life abundantly means, although I was recently offered a man's hand in marriage, a man with a net worth of several million dollars. However, he asked me to do the one thing I could NOT do: forsake my faith in Jesus. He said that when I gave up my faith, we could get married and live happily ever after. Not a chance. Happily ever after is knowing my offspring and I will one day be in heaven—now that's everlasting! For many money is their god, but it can't buy them happiness or health and it can't buy their way into heaven nor prevent their soul from being cast into everlasting hell.

Satan tried this same temptation with our Lord, Jesus Christ. In Matthew 4:8–9 ESV we read, *"Again, the devil took him to a very high mountain and showed him all the kingdoms of the world and their glory. And he said to him, 'All these I will give you, if you will fall down and worship me.'"* But Jesus demonstrated how we are to respond, *"Then Jesus said to him, 'Be gone, Satan! For it is written, You shall worship the Lord your God and him only shall you serve.'"* (Matthew 4:10 ESV)

A Match Not Made in Heaven

"Do not be unequally yoked with unbelievers."

2 Corinthians 6:14 ESV

There is a reason God gave us the instructions not to marry unbelievers. He knew it could be a recipe for disaster. I was given a glimpse of that disaster and hell on earth in my first marriage. It started when I was eighteen and a man put his tongue in my mouth. I just assumed I was pregnant. Well, I made that man marry me so that I wouldn't end up like my mother. Due to a lack of knowledge about how my own body worked, I made a huge mistake at a young age. The beginning of my marriage was okay. I wasn't actually pregnant when I got married; however, soon after I ended up becoming pregnant. By the age of twenty, I had two children—a girl and a boy.

This leads to the moment when my kids were two and three. My husband thought it would be funny to put a tab of acid in my root beer. His friend had the same idea, yet neither knew the other had put a tab in my drink. Both were stoned to the bone and thinking that this Christian woman needed to get loose. Three days later, I woke up in the Fort Hood Army Hospital where my milkman dropped me and my two babies off. The hospital staff walked me around the clock for three days and nights, hoping I would finally wake, not knowing what had happened to me.

The precious moment in this scenario is that my three-year-old daughter was able to wiggle out of the partially open bedroom door to open the front door for the milkman and tell him her mommie can't wake up. I was lying in their closet while her two-year-old brother was crying over me. Our milkman pushed the bedroom door open which was being blocked by a dresser and placed the three of us in his milk truck and took us to the emergency room. Who knew the milkman would hear the cries of Songbird, my little girl, saying her mommie would not wake up? The milkman let himself in and rescued my little family and me. It's a sad thing that a husband and father would leave his family alone knowing their mother was unconscious with two little people who couldn't feed themselves. I still can't believe that he would leave his babies locked behind a bedroom door and only come home after his shift at the Army job. Had he just hoped everything would be all right? Was he thinking that I would wake up and clean up the mess from last night's party? How could he place a tab of acid in his young wife's drink and think everything would be all right for his two young babies? Obviously he wasn't thinking at all! When I regained consciousness, I was being helped up by two orderlies slowly walking me. I didn't know where I was or why I was in this facility until I could remember the last thing that happened to me, my husband handing me a can of root beer.

The doctor said that I would probably have flashbacks for the rest of my life and that I may never be normal again. I do know I experienced hell, the colors, the screams and the faces of anguish and death, reaching for help and no one seeming to hear, reaching to get out of that dark place but there was no footing, no ceiling, no flooring, just aimless darkness and gnashing of teeth and the fires I couldn't see but could feel... it was hell.

Shortly after I told my story to the MPs and doctors, I was given a clean bill of health and my belongings were shipped to San Diego. I had money, my two babies, and a fresh start. I prayed every day as I drove from Texas to California asking God to heal me and not allow flashbacks or anything which Satan meant for bad to harm my little family and me.

Just being able to pray is a precious moment. Having God answer those prayers is beyond amazing! I have never had a flash back!

My now ex-husband always denied what happened during that season of our young married life, but the commander of Fort Hood would surely remember. His military unit was quick to help get me on the road and moved to San Diego to get away from him and his abuse. The trip did not include my husband. My husband was not my responsibility. He was the military's problem now and I did not see him through this ordeal. I really don't know what happened to his career after that, and I honestly didn't care. My train of thought was to just try and survive the horrible memories of the abuse and the health issues for the sake of my two little children and myself.

But even through this hell, I clung to Jesus as my father. My husband beat me. He was physically and emotionally abusive, yet I always knew I was God's girl and He wouldn't allow me to fail. He picked me up, cleaned me up, and put me back on my feet again. Just as Jesus endured the cross and rose again, I would also rise above this hell on earth.

When I got to California, I wanted to find a way to make something of myself. I had two little people counting on me so it wasn't going to be easy. I enrolled in college! It was a struggle being a single parent with two little mouths to feed, but the thought of those two precious children who were now woven into my life gave me motivation. I couldn't fail—it wasn't an option. If I had faith the size of a mustard seed, I could do anything! That concept from one of the Bible verses that Mrs. H often quoted really stayed with me. Another powerful verse is *"For with God nothing is impossible."* (Luke 1:37 NKJV)

A Dear John from God

*"For I will be merciful to their unrighteousness, and their sin
and their lawless deeds I will remember no more."*

HEBREWS 8:12 NKJV

Have you ever received a "Dear John" letter from anyone? I got one
from God!

I will never forget it or it's lesson. No one could have taught me a
lesson in that moment of heartache and torment except Him.

I lost John. It was one of my hardest life lessons. My whole life I
waited for someone to love me and appreciate the good girl I was and
the talented woman I became. I was proud of my many accomplishments
as an arc welder, an eighteen-wheel truck driver, a law firm and hospital
manager, a men's correctional officer, Realtor, Pastor, and a single mom
who put herself through college. Plus I had and endured nearly a dozen
foster homes; and that stint with the Native American rights march across
the United States.

I was expecting to have a superhero husband; or at the very least,
a mate. So I battled with my mind and heart why God hadn't sent me a
"special someone." One night, my children were tucked in bed and I was
getting ready for the next day. I was making the kids' lunches, setting
clothes out for school, and cleaning the kitchen. I had the radio on in the

living room listening to music. Music gave me the extra burst of energy to get over the hump and help me forget how tired I really was at the end of the day.

I remember this as if it happened last night.

I was washing dishes and my music stopped. The first thing I did was look at the clock to see if it was midnight. In those days the music stopped on the radio channels at midnight; yet it was only around ten. I went to my living room where the stereo was located and paused at the doorway to see if it was going to come back on. It didn't, so I approached the radio and just as I reached for the dial, a loud, powerful voice came on and said, "I am bringing you a tall, dark, and handsome man who will love you and your children!" Then the music continued. I was awestruck. I knew that was a voice from heaven giving me an answer to my prayer. God interrupted my radio station to talk to me and He knew I would go to the radio and adjust the dial. His perfect timing. I know it's hard for some to believe but God had to speak through a donkey once in the Bible. I don't own a donkey but a radio. The message was loud and clear. He promised to answer my prayer.

Remember He gives us the desires of our heart if we put Him first above all things? *"Delight yourself in the LORD, and He will give you the desires of your heart."* (Psalm 37:4 NIV) Do I think that means He will give us anything and everything we ask for? No. But He changes the desires of our heart to fit his good and perfect will. And He delights in every detail of our lives. *"The Lord directs the steps of the Godly. He delights in every detail of their lives."* (Psalm 37:23 NLT). I am a believer and know He numbers every hair on my head so I have no doubt He knows when I need an answer.

I worked at Wilderness Industries where I was the utility person building up travel trailers. I was one of their heavyweights so to speak. I mean not every man could do all the things I was gifted with, such as laying carpet, welding frames, hanging curtains, replacing windows and doors, and so forth. I was the person who would work any department and be the best at it. When Friday came around I was exhausted but I still had to put on my single-parent hat and be Supermom. Supermom didn't own a car. I had a bicycle and two children in elementary school. Supermom picked them up on her bike and went to McDonald's for a Friday treat. One child sat on the handlebars and the other sat on the back fender. We were off like a dirty shirt.

Before I bought a washing machine, one kid carried a load of laundry on the back of the bike, and the one on the handlebars carried a bag of groceries. It was a treat for them and a good workout for me. Every once in a while someone in a passing car would yell out some sly remark. The best remark I ever heard was, "You look like a Volkswagen without its shell." It was a glorious life and the three of us really looked forward to Friday at McDonald's. Friday night was also the night I sometimes liked to go out by myself, but couldn't because I had no car.

There was a car dealership near where I used to cross over the railroad tracks with my two little kiddos. A salesman told me that if I had a job, he could sell me a car on credit. All I needed was a little down payment. Soon it would be rainy season again and a car would be a nice comfort. Then perhaps I could find a local church, and I also wouldn't be left with so many chores to do on a Sunday night to get ready for another workweek. During the next few weeks, I saved my bonus checks from Wilderness and bought myself a Chevy Malibu. I felt like I owned a Mercedes-Benz.

On this particular Friday I decided to reward myself and go out, of course after our family treat at McDonald's. I put the kiddos to bed, had my friend Margaret's daughter come over to babysit, and away I went from my HUD home in San Joaquin to Dos Palos where my biological mother and father still lived. I thought I might bump into one of them and let them see what an awesome woman I turned out to be.

I parked my car outside of a local bar where my mother was well known and rolled my car windows down so I could hear the music and listen for my mother's voice. She could get real loud inside the bars after a few drinks and she had a high-pitched laugh. She danced from bar to bar on the main street of Dos Palos. Sure enough, I could hear her voice but didn't want her to see me in my car. I just wanted to witness if she was still the same Lupe that didn't raise me and chose the bar scene rather than my two brothers and me.

As the saying goes, "Same ole, same ole." I watched as she moved from bar to bar with several men and women. With my body hunched down so she couldn't see me, I looked in my rear view mirror and side mirrors. Another man was following her, or following the men with her and he noticed me in my car.

He stopped by my passenger window and asked if I needed any help. I said, "No, thank you." And he continued into the bar where my mother was. He finally came out before my mother exited and asked again if I needed any help. I right away thought he was just like all the other men in the bars, trying to pick up a woman. I am sorry if I am offending anyone but that's the truth. If he was following my mother—and she was known for putting out—surely he was looking for that type woman.

This time I told him, "I am sitting in my car watching my mother bar-hop."

He said, "And I am watching my father bar-hop. Who is your mother?"

I said, "Lupe."

Instantly his face turned into a smirk. He said, "My father is the man she is with, Junior."

I got a smirk on my face, too. I immediately didn't like his father because my mother was being used by Junior. Yet that was what this young man thought of my mother. She was using his dad. We both laughed and realized we had something in common even if we didn't like each other's parent.

He asked me out for at a drink or a cup of coffee. I thought, *He probably thinks I am like my mother and I am easy like her.* I made it impossible for him to see me and told him, "If you want to see me, you can meet me and my children at church any Sunday."

He said, "I would love to. Can you give me the address?"

Really? He wanted an address? All I gave him was the name of the church in San Joaquin, 36 miles away and the start time of its worship service.

I never expected him to show up and didn't want to know him anyway. What kind of son could come from a heathen of a father, anyway? Does the Bible verse "*Judge not, that ye be not judged*" (Matthew 7:1 KJV) come to mind?

I forgot about him and his personal invitation to my church and into my world. Not even my mother or father would drive 36 miles to visit my brothers and me when we were in foster homes; and surely this strange man wouldn't either. Yet there he stood behind me, trying to surprise me as I was walking into my church entrance. He called my name, "Hi, Charli! Remember me?"

I looked at him and realized how tall, dark, and handsome he was. I didn't get that view a few nights ago on the streets of Dos Palos. But this morning when I turned around to someone calling my name, I saw him for the very first time. Really?! Wow! What a handsome hunk of a man. He must have been 6'5" and 180 lbs., Levi denims, and wide shoulders. He bent down to shake the hands of my son and daughter and then he asked permission to sit with us.

I don't know if I was embarrassed or shy or whatever this feeling was that came over me. It was the first time I was caught off guard and was speechless—perhaps the word was *flabbergasted*. But I sensed this man, John, wanted more than me. He also wanted my children.

I didn't greet him with a kiss, just a friendly hug. I wanted him to know I was nothing like my mother so I attempted to keep him at a distance. I hoped he would climb my mountain of fear and mistrust and show me he wanted all of me, including my two little children. Then perhaps I could trust him for a kiss someday.

John was faithful and met us at church for a month of Sundays. I had kept a family tradition I learned at the foster home and had an afternoon Sunday dinner of home-cooked fried chicken, mashed potatoes, corn, and iced tea. My children prompted me to invite John, so I did.

John spent more time with my children than he did with me. That was fantastic. Watching this interaction allowed me to begin letting my guard down and start trusting him. We never slept together and spending the night at my house would never happen as long as I wasn't married. I didn't want the neighbors or my children to get the "appearance of evil," as the Bible calls it. Even if John and I spent the entire day together, when the night fell he had to make the 36 mile drive home.

He was persistent in his trips to see us on Sundays although he had never been in a church until he met us. He loved hearing the stories of Jesus and my life and I loved telling them to him. He was amazed that I was Lupe's daughter as I was nothing like her—that was a compliment. John kept telling me he had a big surprise for me. It felt like the kind of surprise when a man was going to ask for your hand in marriage, but that wasn't it. He had already asked me that and I couldn't commit. Although I was separated from my children's father, I was still legally married. Had I been divorced, I would have happily said yes to John. As for the surprise, he said it wasn't quite ready and I would have to wait.

I called his home once; his mother answered and was so excited to hear my voice. She wanted me to know how John's life was impacted since he met me and how happy they were for him. She said he seemed so calm since he started going to our church. She said the friends he'd grown up with didn't even recognize this new John had changed for the good! He even looked forward to working more and seeing us more. He had to drop a few of his friends because he didn't appreciate any snide remarks concerning his new girlfriend with a package of kids he wasn't responsible for. To John, I was the woman God brought into his world— the woman he had waited for all his life. His mother couldn't wait to meet me and her new grandchildren whom she would love to spoil on their ranch in Dos Palos.

Unfortunately, I was having a few financial challenges and took the bait to make some easy money. I am absolutely, one hundred percent, sure it was the design of Satan to turn me away from John and my potential future and think about this money adventure. Truthfully, it had never crossed my mind that John was the man God told me was coming soon—the tall, dark, and handsome man who would love my children and me. I was too busy living to listen to God. I didn't spend morning time or any time alone with Jesus—just church on Sunday, my weekly duty—and trying to be a good example for my children. I was busy watching John play with my children. I was busy looking pretty, busy being a single mom, busy being a breadwinner. I didn't consider that voice on my radio, not one single time until much later.

At Wilderness Industries where I was an arc welder I worked mostly with men. I had discovered that men didn't typically have wicked tongues and gossip behind folks' backs. Men seemed to be straight up and I loved my working environment. However, in those days not all men were used to working with a woman. My first week at Wilderness Industry, my boss told me he might have to move me, not that I wasn't a good arc welder, but because the men were not doing their work when I was around. They were apparently "distracted." So I became a "utility worker" making the same wage using my talents in various other areas. The work was hard but rewarding.

I had a friend named Stu who was also an arc welder. We had been out on a few dates but at this point, we were just friends. We both worked super hard and needed a night out, just chilling and having fun. He asked if I wanted to spend an evening cruising the streets of San Joaquin in his lowrider, playing music. I did enjoy his company and I didn't have any plans for Friday, so I said yes.

He picked me up and also paid for my kids' babysitter. Stu and I dressed up like Bonnie and Clyde. He wore a large hat and I wore a mink stole wrap. We looked good sitting in his low rider. Yes, we drank a little Boonsboro wine and smoked a joint before strolling the streets. I didn't do any of those things with John. I didn't want John to think of me as anyone other than a saint and good mother for sure—no hint of my mother in me.

As we were laughing and singing and cruising, Stu said if I ever needed to make a few hundred extra bucks on a weekend, he could arrange it. All I had to do was deliver a suitcase for one of his friends who was out of the country. It sounded harmless and very beneficial to me. Plus, I would take an airplane trip to San Francisco, charge up some credit cards, get a room for the weekend, and wait for the suitcase to be picked up. No problem.

I trusted Stu and he knew how much my children meant to me—as least that is what I thought. I was so gullible! I took his word as gospel and didn't consider that I was sitting with a man in his lowrider, drinking wine, smoking a joint (both of which were illegal) and yet I trusted him? Why would I think he was legit? Why would I trust him? Why did he seem like a sweet, innocent lamb? I didn't really know the Bible in those days. If I did, I might have recognized him as a wolf in sheep's clothing.

I was nervous as Friday approached. I needed a babysitter for the weekend so I talked to my friend Margaret. Her daughters would babysit my children. I told her about this job in which I could make a couple hundred dollars, plus all the other carrots that were luring me in. She told me straight up, "Girlfriend, you are going to carry drugs for them!" What a surprise to me! Truly I was shocked by this revelation! I wouldn't get into trouble if I didn't know what I was carrying, right? Wrong! I would be an accomplice to this crime.

I decided at the last minute I wasn't going to do it. I told Stu but he said I would have to meet a man who was the solicitor of this transaction that evening and tell him to his face. Why would I have to meet him? Stu told me that after I met him, he would understand why I was pulling out; that because of my children and my innocent self (I looked that part) he would let me off the hook. Truly, I didn't understand any of this new scene. But I couldn't let Stu down. After all, he was the "friend" who set me up!

I couldn't tell John. I could only confide in Margaret. She was my very best friend and I was her very first white girl friend. She wouldn't let me in her house for nearly a year just because I was white. I am ashamed to say, but I did quite a lot of teeter tottering across the line of good and evil at this point in my life. This was one of those nights of evil where God forgave me, but I still reaped what I had sown.

I met the middle-aged man at a hotel. He let me into his room and asked me a few questions about the arrangements I had committed to and I basically told him I was scared and didn't want to do anything which might get me into trouble with the law, especially because of my children.

He told me it wasn't that easy to back away: I would have to prove to him that I wasn't a person who was with the police and I needed to take my clothes off. What? How would that prove anything? Did he think I was wearing a wire? I felt scared like I did when I was five years old and my cousin wanted to give me 7-up as he unzipped his pants. This fat man was unzipping his pants, too. And at that moment I knew I had made many mistakes leading to this point. I didn't trust my instinct to run. I took off my clothes except my bra and underwear and he pushed me back until I fell on the bed. His disgusting self all over me, I was frozen and couldn't move: I was becoming a prostitute just like my mother.

I had walked myself right into this mess. Could I have called it rape? Not exactly. But I didn't want him. Because of my stupidity, I put myself in the devils' den and got into bed with the devil and when this disgusting man wanted me to give in, I snaked my way from underneath him and told him to give me a minute to go to the bathroom. He did, and I got my clothes on and told him I was leaving. He told me to take the fifty-dollar bill on the dresser. I knew if I did I was a prostitute.

I returned home and felt filthy. I was filthy. It was too early to go to bed, but that is what I wanted to do—hide in my bedroom after a long shower. Just as I lay down, John called and told me he was in town working and could he stop by just to catch a nap? He said he had been working all day and was totally exhausted and although he knew that I don't allow men to sleep over, he just needed a brief nap and didn't know anyone else.

I of course told him, "No, John. Do you know what the neighbors would think?" What a big hypocrite I was and John didn't want to break my heart or rules, so he drove home to Dos Palos and I fell asleep. Around 3:00 AM I woke up to a dream, I thought. His mother called me to tell me John had been in an accident. I hung the phone up. I still thought I was dreaming. Then my phone rang again. It was his mother. She told me John was hit head on by a semi as John had fallen asleep at the wheel. He pulled into a semi and had put his foot through his floorboard of his little VW bug trying to put the brakes on. He died instantly. I didn't believe her. I called Margaret and had her call John's mother to be sure I wasn't having a nightmare because of the traumatic other things that happened that same night. Maybe I was having a nightmare. But my friend Margaret made the call and found out that John was dead.

My "Dear John" letter from God. God took John that night. Only God has the power of life and death. He had brought me the perfect gift for my children and me but I forsook Him and turned my back on my whole life's lesson of "not becoming like my mom."

I didn't want to live another day. I didn't care about anything except finding John. I just knew if I could find him, I could pray him back into life. I called his mother and asked where John was. She told me they took his body to San Francisco. I didn't believe her. I could feel his presence. I drove to the scene but there was nothing except skid marks. I drove to the local mortuary and could sense John was in there but no one would let me in. The local sheriff knew John and also knew of me but he told me John wasn't there.

If I couldn't bring John back to life, I wanted to die and be buried with him. I didn't consider my kids at the time—my grief and pain were bigger than me. I had never experienced such anguish. I had met with his mother earlier that day before the drive into the mortuary and she let me go into John's room so I could find something that had his scent on it. I selected his worn Levi's, which I found and wore around my neck. She guided me to the surprise he had been working on for my children and me: he had several detailed drawings of the home he was going to build.

I felt his death was my fault. He had begged me for a nap but I said, "It looks bad, John, no." And earlier that very evening I was in the act of prostitution. What a big hypocrite. I was drenched in tears and snot and didn't care about anything except to be with John. I didn't realize how much I loved him until I didn't have him anymore.

That evening I parked at the mortuary, no other cars around except mine. I planted my body near a window. I knew with all my heart that John's body was in there. I cried and loudly grieved. I couldn't help myself. I was so sorry, so sad. I had been so unappreciative of the gift God gave me—all the love John had shown my children and me. I begged God for a second chance and to bring him back to life like He did Lazarus—but He wouldn't, didn't, and there I lay outdoors wailing.

I heard a gentle voice say, "Charli, would you like to come in and I will light a fire?"

I wiped my face to see who was speaking. He said, "I was John's friend and he spoke of you day and night. You know, Charli, if it wasn't for you, John wouldn't be in Heaven right now. You changed John's life. You were the only person who ever taught him or spoke to him about Jesus Christ and he definitely is with Jesus." That mortician is the only person who said anything that caught my attention. No one else said anything that was meaningful; but this one man spoke of Jesus and my hope was restored instantly. Just the name Jesus turned on a light in my heart, my mind, and I knew God would forgive me and He had taken John home to be with Him.

I can't say if I had chosen differently that night and had not gone to the motel or listened to the voice of Satan speaking through a so-called friend, John and I would be living happily ever after. But I can say I learned a strong lesson that night: if you play in the mud, you get dirty and if you stay in the mud you'll stay dirty. I chose rather than to be bitter, to be better and let that event be a lesson for me: Never again entertain those disgusting opportunities to make fast money, don't listen to so-called friends who knowingly break the law and want to lead you down the wrong path, don't ever consider doing anything my mother used to do, and to tell my children this story when they were older so they could hopefully learn from my mistakes.

My son asked me many times whatever happened to John and all I could say was he died; but there was so much more to the story and the events which led to his death.

Did God forgive me? Yes. Have I forgiven myself? Somewhat yes. Does God bring it up again? No. I have—only because God wanted me to write about Dear John.

I heard, "Charli, write this Dear John story." And so I have—yet I have to be honest that I fear as I reveal my sin openly in this story there will be some who will disown me as their Christian friend. For those who will judge me, perhaps this story is not for you. Rather it is meant for someone who the Holy Spirit is reaching for, someone who needs to know that our Father is a Father who forgives. He sees us each moment of our life and already knows our sins. All He asks of us is to repent. 1 John 1:9 KJV promises, *"If we confess our sins, He is faithful and just to forgive us our sins and to cleanse us from all unrighteousness."* He forgives us even though the world may not. He forgives us because Jesus already paid the penalty. Romans 3:22–24 NIV says, *"This righteousness is given through faith in Jesus Christ to all who believe. There is no difference between Jew and Gentile, for all have sinned and fall short of the glory of God, and all are justified freely by his grace through the redemption that came by Christ Jesus."* How can this be? Because God loves us! *"For God so loved the world that he gave his only begotten Son, that whosoever believeth in him should not perish, but have everlasting life."* (John 3:16 KJV)

A CHRISTMAS GIFT OF LOVE

"Every good and perfect gift is from above, coming down from the Father of the heavenly lights, who does not change like shifting shadows."

JAMES 1:17 NIV

In His presence we shine. There is no shortage of light or love there, and even in the darkest moments of our life He still shines. He is the precious moment! His light and love guide us out of our darkness and dungeons toward hope and He allows us to love and forgive because He loves and forgives us!

Sometimes people ask me about my moms and I love to share this story about Mrs. H. Because of her past, many may think she was the worst and unforgivable. Yet, if God loved her and forgave her, then perhaps I should too. God made that possible.

I wanted her to know I was nothing like my original mother and I was a good girl. What Satan meant for my harm ... I was confident that one day I could prove myself and pay my respects to her and Dad. I wanted to visit her and Dad and show off my two children while they sat on my lap as I loved them. Something she never did, love and caress. I wondered when I sat in her presence with my love overflowing onto my children if she would consider where that affection came from. Certainly she didn't teach affection yet you could say 'my cup runneth over' with love and one day I hoped to show her that I loved her too.

That day came, with an opportunity to write a play about my childhood under Mr. and Mrs. H's roof during Christmas seasons. However, I would leave all the bad parts out and have the opportunity to thread Jesus into an elementary school Christmas party and play. One school year, my preschooler, Strongwind, and first grader, Songbird, came home from school disheartened. I could see it on their faces. Both had a note pinned to their shirts when I picked them up. I saw the yellow paper attached to them and immediately thought they were either in trouble, had head lice, or there was an infectious disease at their school. I felt upset simply because they were.

At this time of our life, our only transportation was a bicycle. I was proud to pedal them to and from school. Other children thought my kiddos were lucky because their mom rode them on a bike. Strongwind and Songbird would take turns on the handlebars and back fender position. But before we got on the bicycle today, I needed to handle their sad faces and that note which was causing them stress. We sat at the school curb, both my kiddos beside me, and I took off those notes. As I read the notes, I realized the bad news would ruin any kid's day.

There would be no Christmas in school. This year it was cancelled! How could that be? Who in the administration would to do such a thing? Public school or not this was just unheard of at the time. I needed to get to the bottom of this asap. I would find a way around this disaster ... 'no Christmas' was certainly not an option.

Luckily, I was on the PTA committee which was meeting that week. All the parents seemed to show up for this PTA meeting as all their children were sad and crying about 'No Christmas.' Come to find out this old school's auditorium did not pass health and safety inspections and was being shut down until further notice; therefore there was no place to have a Christmas performance, at least not this particular year. From preschool to sixth grade, kids and parents alike, no one cared why there was no Christmas party. They wanted a remedy to fix Christmas and so did I. That night after the PTA meeting when Strongwind and Songbird went to bed, we knelt beside their bunkbed and asked God to please fix Christmas, amen!

A bright light turned on in my head and I was certain this idea could save Christmas for our school. Our school principal didn't like the situation either but he didn't have any recommendations on how to resolve the problem. He was open to any suggestion to save this important season in his school. I met with him and asked if another school offered their cafeteria or auditorium for our kids, was it possible he could authorize our Christmas party to be performed there? His first response was yes, but then he started with kids practicing and transportation and risk and on and on and on... I understood his position and realized our dilemma. But another brilliant light went off in my head. Perhaps the children's parents could perform for their children this year and surprise their children with a secret performance that would make Christmas even more enchanting.

I requested a special PTA meeting as soon as the principal gave me a thumbs up and half the parents showed up. Two PTA meetings back-to-back was unheard of, but parents wanted a remedy and if I had the solution, they were in line to fix their children's Christmas.

The solution was the parents would perform on stage instead of their children. We would also surprise the kids with Santa Claus who would show up at this other school where the parents would perform. The parents wanted to know what they were going to perform. None of them were speakers, singers, artist, just parents who wanted their children to have a good Christmas.

When this PTA meeting was over, we had committed parents who would give time, money, or whatever necessary to fulfill Christmas. Aww, a sigh of relief for the kiddos but now the hard part; what were we going to perform? And was there a school which would loan their cafeteria? I like to say, "When God opens a door, He doesn't turn around and slam it in your face." However, you have to walk through it. Just like the Israelites when they were escaping from Egypt: the Lord opened the Red

Sea, but the children of God had to step into it. Well, we were at the Red Sea moment. Like the Israelites, we had to move forward.

Since I opened my mouth at the first PTA meeting, I was the spearhead for this project and everyone was looking to me for the answers, meanwhile I was looking at my children and God for answers. Why my kids? Because of their little faces which prayed with me for answers with the faith of a little child! We were hoping for a Christmas miracle to save the school Christmas. I called a local school and spoke to their principal. It was a school where my brothers and I had attended. The principal gave us the green light! We now had a performance area, performers, volunteers, and staff approvals. Teachers were relieved as they would be able to continue the Christmas tradition in the classrooms. But my dilemma was how would it all tie together? I wanted to include Mr & Mrs. H and of course Jesus.

It was really quite simple: now that I had all the ingredients, all I had to do was write a Christmas play where the whole school and parents participated. In spite of the fact that I had no clue what I was doing or history involving theatrics, once the Lord turned the lights on I was aglow! A story came into my heart of Mrs. H and how Christmas was all about the gift of baby Jesus and the Bible story of His birth. Mrs. H always sat in her rocking chair while we gathered around her dressed in our pajamas. She read about that first Christmas from the Bible and we listened intently. Then we hopped directly into bed and went right to sleep because that was the night Santa would drop down our chimney to bring us toys if we were good children.

That gave me the idea: parents would perform that moment on stage. Parents would be the children in their pajamas sitting at Mrs. H's feet. Mrs. H being performed by one of the parents and as she read the Christmas story of Jesus' birth from the Bible; the nativity scene and Wise Men would be performed by parents walking through the cafeteria from the back to the foot of the stage. As she finished reading the Christmas story, the parents (children) would jump into bed excited for Santa Claus to arrive.

The night of the Christmas play, all the children from our school sat as close as possible to the front in order to watch their parents perform. They were especially exuberant as there was a rumor Santa Claus might show up too! Since the story was written about them, Mr. and Mrs. H were my special guests for this Christmas school performance. They had the guest of honor seats and arrived on time dressed up in their Sunday go-to-meeting attire.

While writing this play, I was a full time student in junior college. My college participated as well as the fire department and local stores who donated one toy per child. The entire stage props had been created in the classrooms unbeknown to the children, and the costumes were donated by my college. The fire department brought the hay for the manger and made sure we had their presence in case Santa's reindeer needed help.

I auditioned college students for Santa and the gentleman my heart chose was going through a hopeless season in his life but wanted to participate in this adventure in anyway, not necessarily Santa. My heart told me to choose him. His heart filled with joy when he slid down the chimney on stage and looked at all the children's faces who cried and yelled 'Santa Claus!' Santa's three huge bags also dropped through the chimney which one classroom had created for our Christmas surprise night. The children on stage (parents) rubbed their eyes as they awoke to Santa's ruckus. However, they couldn't get out of bed until Mom came in to wake them up. They listened as Santa Claus called names from packages he pulled from his sack. When Santa read a name, it was not of a child/ parent on stage but of a child in the audience. Of course the children in the audience didn't expect their names to be called: they were watching the performance of their parents, thinking Santa was bringing gifts to the children on stage. Santa scratched his as if confused that perhaps he had dropped down the wrong chimney. As Santa called names of kids sitting in the audience they suddenly started jumping up from their seats excitedly yelling, It's me, it's me!"

The night ended with each child receiving a gift and a picture with Santa on stage. It was a family affair and the parents agreed it was the best Christmas they ever experienced in school or home. They got the pat on the back—they made it happen. I just listened to that small voice in my heart and obeyed. That night honored Mr. and Mrs. H, blessed a young man who was our Santa, blessed our children, and blessed their parents with the Christmas story. Some had never heard the Christmas story before but they all heard it that night!

At the beginning of this night's event, we had music being performed until everyone took their seats. The entertainer sang a popular song at the time, "Father and Son" by Cat Stevens. which was a popular song at the time. If I hadn't known better, I would have guessed our performer was the identical twin to Cat Stevens. My son, Strongwind, who was a preschooler, remembers this performance and song. He still sings it to this day, always referring to the first time he heard it at this Christmas Play. Blessed memories!

Why do I write this story? To acknowledge what Satan meant to do was destroy lives in this foster home of hell, but God turned it around for His glory and for such a time as this. Did Mr. and Mrs. H have any other child or foster child acknowledge them in public or give them credit for their attempt to do the best they could with what they knew? I don't know. I do know when God is in the house there is light, love, faith, hope, and also long-suffering.

I cannot condone the hardship thrust upon any of us at any age, but I can understand that if Christ is in us, we will have the resurrected spirit that loves all the time no matter what the circumstances. *"He who is in you is greater than he who is in the world"* (1 John 4:4 NKJV) and I might add, definitely greater than I am myself.

Although I didn't have time to walk Mr. and Mrs. H out, they knew I had written the story about them. They got to enjoy the delight of all the children and I believe they felt the love. I don't recall seeing Mom and Dad after that night as I had relocated to SLO to attend Cal Poly, but heard some years later that Mr. H had passed away and Mrs. H was moved to a Reno, Nevada, nursing home. I hoped to visit them one more time after I graduated from college so I could show them what I had accomplished despite my past, but it didn't happen like that. I fell into a position in life which accidentally directed me into Mrs. H's room later in her life. Remember what I said about coincidence—no such thing— God orchestrated yet another **precious moment**!

WHEEL CHAIR MANOR

"I, the Lord, make Myself known to him in a vision; I speak to him in a dream."

NUMBERS 12:6 NKJV

Several years after Cal Poly, I remarried and had another little girl. We named her Ebb-oni which means one sent from above. Her father represented another brutal episode in my life and I had to escape into a shelter for battered women and children. I changed my name, occupation, and relocated to an area where he would never find us. This trauma affected Strongwind, Songbird, and nearly killed Ebb-oni and me. Sometimes as we look at the seeds we sow we may become aware that they have turned into weeds. As parents we must exercise extreme care with which seeds we sow because our children can be caught up in the thistles. In such a case, it may be best to uproot and start all over again in good soil and surroundings.

I moved to a new area. Songbird had been traumatized and was recovering from a rape and an abduction so I stayed close to home hoping I could protect my family from any more turmoil. I waited three years before dating again. I needed that hiatus because trusting any man wasn't possible. I had escaped the hands of Ebb-oni's dad and wasn't anxious to start another relationship. After a few years I started dating a handsome, slow walking, well-educated fellow. The only reason I considered this man, KW, was because I watched him at work for nearly a year and he watched me. We merely smiled at each other and never spoke a word other than greetings.

Eventually he worked up the courage to ask me out. He asked me to take a weekend drive to Reno, a place he had spent a lot of time. I said no to the weekend but yes to Friday after work and back on Saturday. I had a babysitter but I could only afford just one overnight. Ebb-oni was three and Strongwind and Songbird were teenagers. I couldn't count on either one of them to watch Ebb-oni because their lives were pretty busy and unplanned day to day.

I met him at work so he didn't know where I lived as I was very protective of myself and my children. He was okay with this and in fact didn't reveal his home address either. On our way to Reno, he chattered about all the women he had entertained in Reno including his daughters, mother, ex-wife, etc. Somehow this generated a bit more trust, knowing that he took family, people he cared about to this destination. Then came my turn to tell him my stories of foster homes, miracles, visions and dreams which brings me to my dream the night before this trip to Reno. After hearing a few of my stories, he decided it was time for a little break. He pulled his beautiful new black showroom Corvette over at a spot along the road. He had made us a little picnic for the road which included a bottle of wine. The picnic I really appreciated. It was his thoughtfulness that touched me, but that bottle of wine made me wary. My first thought was he intended to get me intoxicated so I would let my guard down. So I told him wine isn't okay unless he was going to drink and I was going to drive his new Corvette.

"Oh no, that's not happening today," he said.

"Good" was my comment.

But then he asked me if I had ever done drugs or LSD. I quickly told him, "No, why do you ask? Do I look like someone who does drugs?"

"No," he said, "but the stories you tell sound like you have been on a steady trip, stuff I have never heard of."

I told him I had a dream last night about a gigantic rocking chair on top of a building and the name on the building was Wheel Chair Manor. KW asked me what I thought the dream meant and I told him I had no clue because I hadn't talked to Jesus about the dream. Now remember KW and I had never had a full conversation before this first date so he was just getting to know me. He wanted to know if I was a Jesus freak kind of person and I said I don't know about freak but I am sure one of Jesus' girls. My response was designed to let him know I wasn't an easy ride – in the Corvette or anywhere else.

I let him know since I moved to this new location I had been raped, my daughter had been abducted, I changed my name because of an abusive husband, and he was my first date since those events. My intent was to draw a picture in his mind that I had been hurt, abused, and would not tolerate another incident which might hint at damaging my family or me.

Evidently all my stories on this six-hour-plus ride caused him some confusion because once we got to Reno, his favorite place to play, he was lost and embarrassed for nearly three hours. Lucky for us he had packed a large picnic so we could eat while lost. I was beginning to question whether he had ever actually been to Reno or whether he was truly lost. He was ashamed as he had no explanation for why he was so lost. I told him to be quiet for a minute and allow me to pray because "Jesus knows we are lost and He can show us a way out of town." He told me to go ahead and pray, although he didn't really do that, but since it works for me, maybe God would help us get out of there and we would go to San Francisco where I wanted to end up. As I was praying God reminded me of the dream I had about Wheel Chair Manor. I could see the rocking chair on top of a building and told KW, "You know what, my foster mother, Mrs. H, moved to Reno Nevada and maybe God wants me to find her while we are here?"

His comment was, "Are you kidding—really?"

My response was "God works in mysterious ways."

Once KW accepted the possibility because of all the other stories I told him, he said, "You know what, Charli, I don't doubt you, because this has never ever happened to me."

Not even five minutes went by and we ended up at a convalescent hospital and there it was—a wheelchair image on top! We both looked at each other like *No way!* I said, "KW, you have to pull over and allow me to ask if she is in there." He did and I went to the front desk and asked if Mrs. H was in their facility. Wouldn't you know it—she was there. I asked if I could please see her as she was my mom for years while I was a child, and they said yes but that she wasn't cognizant and wouldn't even be aware of my presence. I said, "God didn't bring me all this way to pass her by. He wants me to see her."

As I entered her room, nothing was on my mind except to tell her I love her and I forgive her. Her eyes were closed as she lay under her blankets, both arms exposed. I took her left hand, held it and whispered, "Mom, it's Charli. I hope you hear me. I just want you to know I love you and forgive you." She looked over to me and tears ran from her cheek as tears ran from mine and she squeezed my hand.

I also told Mom that I used all the things she taught me, especially about God, and I knew she loved me too. I was done. I knew she heard me and I had freed her from her past. Perhaps now she could rest with Jesus. Or maybe Jesus needed Satan to know he hadn't won, that nothing could separate us from the love of God. It was a **precious moment!**

CAUGHT UP

"In all your ways submit to him, and he will make your paths straight."

PROVERBS 3:6 NIV

What would it take for you to believe in God? Would it take a catastrophe like the great flood in the days of Noah?

Although I do believe in God and His mighty power, I was too busy living life and not really listening to or living for Him until one day a catastrophe struck my life. It stopped me in my tracks as I was hit head-on by a drunk driver. At that moment I was caught up in the sky looking down at my totaled Buick Century with my three-year-old daughter lying on the floor of the passenger side of the car. Sometimes God takes drastic measures to get our attention and set us back on the straight path.

It was October 1986. I can vividly remember the accident as it unfolded. My daughter Ebb-oni was sitting in the front seat with her seat belt on. She was three years old. We had taken this Friday night journey every week for several months. We lived in Bellflower, California, and were headed to my boyfriend's house in Seal Beach on southbound Interstate 405. This was a night devoted to sex, booze, and marijuana when it wasn't legal. Yes, I was a sinner, but this night's plan for sinful activities was stopped short. I know it was the hand of God that stopped me in my tracks.

How could I be a Christian and think that God was okay with my Friday night habits? How was I an example for my daughter? I thought, *How would she know when the bedroom door was shut and she was set up on the couch with her little Cabbage Patch doll, Cheryl, and the cartoon channels on?* My boyfriend was so sweet the way he would tuck Ebb-oni and Cheryl into bed. Then he would turn his attention to me in the bedroom. Although Ebb-oni was only three, she remembers those moments to this day, remembers those moments just like me; and she was only three.

Except for the head-on collision, this particular Friday night was similar to other nights I had with other boyfriends in my life; yet, I wasn't typically so bold as to take my children with me. This time, though, my sights were aimed at having my boyfriend for my husband some day and I wanted to see how he related to my little girl, and to prove to him what an awesome mate I could be.

It had been several months of total commitment to just my boyfriend and his commitment to me. I rationalized that God judges us by the motives of our heart. My line of thinking was, if I had sex exclusively with my boyfriend and he fell in love with me, then perhaps the Lord would excuse my sin because my motive was pure. As I justified my sin, I was ignoring God's Truth. I was listening to Satan's twisting of the truth as I allowed him to influence my decisions. Satan was twisting scripture in my mind, just like when Satan twisted the scripture he quoted to Jesus as he was tempting Him in the wilderness. My plan was to catch this man with my awesomeness; he would propose, we would get married, and everything would be all right. Obviously, that's not how my Father in heaven saw my progression.

There is too much Eve in me—taking God's word and bending it to my satisfaction. I was falling for our corrupt culture's lies that sex outside marriage is okay. Being drunk is okay, being under the influence of drugs is okay, as long as it was legal or I was behind closed doors.

After all, everyone else was doing it. I knew what the Word of God said was happening. "For wide is the gate and broad is the road that leads to destruction," While "small is the gate and narrow the road that leads to life." But I kept rationalizing—Everyone else was doing it which meant it was okay. But it wasn't and God put a halt to it when He allowed a drunk driver to turn his vehicle north into southbound traffic and hit us head on.

My little Ebb-oni was sitting in the front seat buckled up with her doll Cheryl anticipating our visit with my boyfriend. She sang with excitement, ready to be loved by my boyfriend. I had everything packed for Ebb-oni and myself to spend Friday and Saturday night. Ebb-oni had her overnight bag and I had my overnight bag filled with bathing products, perfumes, sexy nightgowns to make my boyfriend want me more, and our favorite cookies.

My boyfriend knew I liked music and he would have the bedroom atmosphere set up with attention to details especially for me. Ebb-oni slept in the living room. This weekend was to be a test. If my boyfriend showed compassion and consideration for Ebb-oni, it told me he loved me and her, too. I was so wrong. I was seeing things as a woman of the world not a Christian woman, and God wasn't accepting my interpretation of His word by capturing a man with my sexuality. I was familiar with the stories of some of the immoral and wicked women I had read about in the Bible; Delilah, Jezebel, the Samaritan woman at the well; none of them were examples I wanted to follow.

There was another female I wouldn't have chosen to follow, my mother. Yet, it was in her footsteps that I was following that night. Her ungodly example was the primary reason that the Lord had NOT allowed me to be raised by her; so I wouldn't become like her! But there I was following a sinful path, creating a godless example for my daughter. I had provoked He put a stop to my intentions and what I was teaching my daughter.

The night was cold and so dark that only taillights shone on the 405 southbound. To my left was the 405 northbound with a cement divider and headlights. Friday evening was thick with traffic as was normal for most Southern California freeways. For a moment, the traffic in front of me seemed to slow down, which made me look ahead and reduce my speed. Then I noticed no taillights, just an oncoming headlight headed full speed toward me. I knew we were going to be hit and instinctively I unfastened our seat belts so I could shove my daughter to the floor. I recall learning at some point that the strongest part of a vehicle was the frame around the front doors and engine and hoped Ebb-oni would survive under the dashboard near the floor frame as I knew if she was seated in the front seat at the time of impact it would kill her.

The next thing I remember, "I was caught up" in the sky looking down at my Buick. I could see two fire engines and paramedics—one pair on my side of my car and another couple of paramedics on Ebb-oni's side of the car. Then I heard the paramedics on my side say, "This one's gone," and the other paramedics on Ebb-oni's side said, "We have a live one."

Immediately the Lord told me, "If I take you home tonight, this is what you will leave your children." He showed me $3,000 in my bank account. I started crying and pleading with the Lord to forgive me as I wanted to leave them much more than that. My whole life was geared around giving my children a home, love, care, an education, and most of all the legacy of a wholesome family. Three thousand dollars was far from that.

Then immediately the Lord showed me a white line drawn on the ground like the white lines on streets to separate traffic. He showed me my life as a young parent. On the right side of the line I was kneeling in prayer at the bedside of my children. Then He showed me on the left side drinking in bars. Then I was back over to the right side walking up the sidewalk to church with my son, Strongwind, and daughter, Songbird. Then again to the left side of the white line—I was rolling a joint and partying with people. I saw myself weaving back and forth between the right and left side of the road. Again I swerved to the right side as I took my children to school. The Lord showed me how the kids always followed me; into school, into grocery stores, into church... They were never in front of me, they were always following me; back and forth across the line, to the right and to the left – the path of right and wrong. It was as if I was instructing my children to "Do as I say and not as I do." I said it was right to pray, right to go to church, right to go to school—all of these actions were good and admirable, but the left side was not good—not a place I wanted my children to follow. All day long nearly every day of my children's lives I told them to hurry up as I taught them to follow my lead, not aware they were watching the wrong behavior too.

Even though I was an adult and all these things were legal, it didn't mean they were good. Those momentary highs and fleeting pleasures were not good seeds to plant and watch develop into healthy trees of life. *"'I have the right to do anything,' you say—but not everything is beneficial. 'I have the right to do anything'—but not everything is constructive."* (I Cor. 10:23 NIV)

While I was traveling back and forth over this white line, it was as simple as standing over a string on the floor. I thought nothing of going dancing at the bars, smoking a few joints on Friday or Saturday night, or getting in bed with men who I thought might love me and give me a future. These actions were as simple for me to do as showing up for church.

I never expected that my children would do such things. After all, I was very careful to hide these actions from them. I didn't consider that my actions were leading them to follow in my footsteps, just as my mother's had led me. Of course I hoped they might follow me into church, prayer and reading God's word, but I would never condone their actions to smoke pot, drink in the bars, or sleep around.

As my out of body experience continued, I turned around to see if my children were behind me. The Lord showed me standing on a white line calling out to Songbird who was in a bar drinking, dancing. I shouted to her, "Let's get going!" But she was too caught up with the bar scene which of course was on the left side of the road, and since she was an adult she let me know she wasn't ready to leave. Then immediately I saw my son, Strongwind, rolling joints and partying with friends. He was standing behind a garage on the left side of the white line passing a joint to his friends—a place where I had wandered and left impressions on his life as I teeter-tottered across the right and wrong side of life's path. As God showed me my children's futures, I realized God was not happy with the example I was setting for my precious gifts. Both Songbird and Strongwind heard me call them, but they were too caught up in their journey through the valley to pay attention to their mom's call. They were adults now and were able to make their own choices. Besides, who was I to tell them it was wrong when I had secretly led the same life?

The Lord knew my heart's desire was to be the best mother and provide a good example for my children—the gifts God gave me—Songbird, Strongwind, and Ebb-oni and $3,000 didn't cut it. Even if I had a house and cars and more money in the bank, I was still not the best example and for sure I was leading them back and forth over the straight and narrow road which is God's way leading to Heaven and then over the wide path which is the way of the world leading to Hell. I never dreamed that one day my daughter would become an addict and an inmate. I couldn't fathom that she would be abducted and pimped out. It never occurred to me that my son would get so caught up in drugs? he would want to commit suicide, quit school, and be under the influence of sexual desires?

I am responsible for where I crossed over the line between what is right and what is wrong. Before I led my three-year-old daughter over the same line, the Lord had had enough. And it was better for Him to stop me that night in my car accident than allow me to lead another life into possible despair. Why didn't I realize the Lord was watching me all this time? Why did I think it would be okay and His grace was sufficient? For one thing, I knew in my heart that nothing could snatch me from the hand of God. I rested in the knowledge that His Grace is sufficient, that I was saved and would one day be in Heaven with the Lord. I thought to myself, "I haven't committed that 'unforgivable sin' so I'm okay." I had first heard about the 'unforgivable sin' from Billy Graham and understood that the only unforgivable sin was rejecting God by turning away from His Holy Spirit... Matthew 12:31 (NIV) says, *"And so I tell you, every kind of sin and slander can be forgiven, but blasphemy against the Spirit will not be forgiven."* Well I thought I hadn't done that, so my little sins were okay, but I was deceiving myself. Perhaps I was listening to that same serpent, Satan, who had whispered to Eve, "Did God really say that?" I guess I was counting on the Lord understanding and still loving and caring about me. But I never ever considered I was leading my children into pits of darkness. I was only considering my life, my walk. Perhaps if I had no children, the Lord might not have allowed that accident that night. I don't know. I do know that I had an encounter with the most High and He caught me up in the sky to have a personal chat and show me the seeds and snares I had planted and walked upon and that I had taken my seed, my children, to those roads of possible doom.

What a beautiful promise we have in the Scripture, *"Surely goodness and mercy shall follow me all the days of my life"* (Psalm 23:6 NKJV) Of course, I wanted my children to follow me where there is goodness and mercy, but there isn't any goodness or mercy from the one who leads us down the road of destruction.

My eldest daughter began encountering that road of destruction at age sixteen: doom, gloom, drugs, sex, prison, homelessness, battered and beaten within an inch of her life. I have seen her through all those horrible episodes, and I know the only times she has been happy and peaceful is when she is serving Jesus. When she walks away from Him and does her own thing, she is never happy and always looking for a fix, which could be anything from a cigarette to an opioid.

My son took a different route and checked himself into rehab. It was successful, thank God, as he has a family of men in his life (my grandsons) who he might have led astray otherwise. The hand of God in the lives of my son and eldest daughter is another book I may write one day, God willing. As for my life, I was given another chance the night I was "caught up" in the sky looking down at my totaled car. That car collision was a wake-up call to me.

Finally, I heard the Lord say, "The best you can give your children is my hand, and if you come over to the right side of the road and stay there, they will eventually follow you." God literally gave me a second chance at life and a new opportunity to alter my ways and become a better role model for my children. I decided the road I was on would change that very night. I realized I must walk on the side of Christ and not teeter-totter so my children would follow me into the light not into the darkness. It was not right away, but I felt certain the Lord was promising me that if I stayed with Him and gave them His hand, He would be faithful and draw them near.

I woke up in the hospital and was determined to never again take my children young or old back and forth. My days of bars, sex, and smoking pot had to stop, and if my boyfriend wanted me in his life, he would have to marry me.

It also occurred to me that giving up those things which I thought brought me momentary joy was like the scripture that states, *"Greater love has no one than this: to lay down one's life for one's friends"* (John 15:13 NIV). I think that would include children too. If I dropped my sinful pleasures to save my children, it was because I love them more than myself and my pleasures. No doubt there are many ways to interpret that Scripture, but when I woke up in the hospital that was the interpretation that came to me. I thought. By giving up my boyfriend and our lustful union I laid down my way of life for the sake of my children. It was my way of taking God's hand and turning my back on the ways of the world.

God had faithfully shown me where I was leading my children! And He was gracious in that my injuries were minor compared to what they could have been. My head went through the windshield when I released my seat belt in order to reach for Ebb-oni's restraint and shove her to the safety of the floor. I lost my ability to stay in my seat. I felt physically ill when I saw my Buick, a few days after the accident. I stood at the driver's side of my totaled car and looked at the windshield's profile. My total facial features; forehead, lips, nose, and chin went through the windshield. It was good to witness the severity of the damage. I realized I could have broken my neck or sustained brain damage if not for God's protection. For years after, I was still taking glass fragments from my forehead and upper hairline. My left leg was bruised but other than that I was okay. It was not the drunk driver's first case and he paid heavily.

When Ebb-oni was lifted out of the Buick, her kneecap was exposed. It was a miracle that not a drop of blood dripped from her wound, nor did she get an infection from the wound. How was that possible? I don't know. How was I caught up in the sky, pronounced dead, yet I woke up in a hospital with a brand-new view of life? Only God saved us that night and gave me another opportunity to serve Him. His grace is sufficient!

Eventually Ebb-oni and I each walked away with a settlement of a few thousand dollars. But more than what we walked away with monetarily, Ebb-oni was left with an L-shaped scar on her left knee as a reminder of God's intervention in our lives. I came away with a second chance; the Lord gave me an opportunity to clean up my life and become a true Christian mother. It was a powerful reminder that I need to stay on the right side of the road and keep holding onto His hand.

The lyrics of a song titled "Faithful" by Eric Nieder speak to the truth of God's faithfulness. I witnessed that faithfulness even when I wandered off course.

Is being caught up, Biblical? You bet! *"I know a man in Christ who fourteen years ago was caught up to the third heaven—whether in the body or out of the body I do not know, God knows."* (2 Corinthians 12:2 ESV)

I completed a study called *"Discerning the Voice of God: How to Recognize When God Speaks"* by Priscilla Shirer. She wrote, *"When He speaks to you internally, and then causes other events to confirm what He's saying…It is likely His sovereign hand orchestrating circumstances to help lead you to His will. When God speaks, He does so persistently."* My take away; when He allows us to see His activity in the circumstances of our lives, we have heard the voice of God. I love that message! I have been hearing the voice of God and witnessing His handiwork since my Holy Communion. It wasn't just a Catholic Holy Communion. For me it was *the Holy Communion* between His Holy Spirit and me. He touched me. He made me His own. He told me I was His kid and He was my Father. *"My son, do not despise the LORD's discipline, and do not resent his rebuke, because the LORD disciplines those he loves, as a father the son he delights in."* (Proverbs 3:11–12 NIV)

How to Love Someone Who Does Not Love You

"If anyone has ears to hear, let him hear." How does that make sense? It's in the reading of God's Word we hear, and faith comes through hearing. The concept of hearing while reading will hopefully make sense and resonate with those who read this story and hear of the hope available through Christ in the midst of their storm.

I am not a professional nor do I have all the answers on how to love someone who does not love you. I am, however, a walking testimony of one who God saw through child abuse, spousal abuse, parental abuse, family abuse, and workplace harassment. He taught me how to forgive, pray for, and eventually love those who spitefully used me. For those who have experienced any of these abuses or perhaps another of life's storms, know that God's mighty hand is reaching down to you. I pray that as you read about some of my experiences and my **precious moments in hell**, you are refreshed with the knowledge and hope that through your hellish circumstances God can and will help. Look for His provisions of

precious moments amidst your storms and see how God can, through your experiences teach you to forgive and love others.

Only God knows the heart. But Satan knows how to push our buttons and twist our minds to the point of despair. Satan derives satisfaction keeping us down in the dumps where we feel inadequate, unacceptable, unloved, and unworthy.

Perhaps you don't have the strength to love or even know what it looks like because you are in the pit of despair—a darkness where only God can see. Yet deep in your heart you are filled with a desire to love and be loved. Perhaps it isn't a personal relationship but a work situation where you are struggling. You may be giving your all, yet doors are slammed in your face. For whatever reason you are not chosen for the job, the team, the promotion. They don't like your kind. You don't fit in.

When I went to work at the men's prison in northern California. I was met with opposition on my first day. The watch commander wanted to meet me on my way into the prison and measure me up. In other words, he wanted to see not only what I looked like but what I was made out of. His first question and comments were, "So you think you want to be a prison guard? Well, I am sending you into 'D' quad where we house the Delta Donuts. They are inmates known for their horrendous crimes and must be sedated. They will make you or break you!"

When the watch commander said, "make me or break me." I thought to myself, *No one is going to make me or break me!* I didn't walk into this prison thinking I had muscle or a physical fight in me; I walked into this prison and occupation because God opened this door and He wanted me to serve Him in this prison. I knew that if God was for me, who could be against me.

Truthfully, the only strength I've ever had was in knowing I was the daughter of my Father, my Lord Jesus Christ, and no one has ever, ever been in my corner except Him. I don't own a black belt except the one I put on for my correctional officer uniform, but I proudly wear a shield constantly. I never take it off even when I sleep. That shield extinguishes all the flaming arrows the evil one shoots at me. I'm referring to the armor of God in Ephesians 6:10–18. *"Above all, taking the shield of faith with which you will be able to quench all the fiery darts of the wicked one."* (Ephesians 6:16 NKJV)

Whenever I was on duty, if a fight broke out I would run to it. I knew the policy, no hostage negotiations, but it was my job to keep the peace.

Right away I learned which notorious inmates were housed in MPNC. Those inmates didn't like me. Honestly, no one liked the female officers inside the prison walls, not even the other officers. The male officers considered the female officers to be a physical liability. One reason was they didn't think we had the muscle to back them up. Another was that the inmates had nothing else to do but dream and fantasize. That wasn't the case with me though as I became known as Ms. Rambo or the Royal Witch of the yard. That was a good thing, it kept the inmates away from me. What scared me in this profession was not the inmates but rather some of the officers who wore the same uniform.

One particular sergeant was especially hateful toward me. For six weeks, the other officers under his command went along with his behavior. He supervised the gun tower officers on the graveyard (11:00 PM–7:00 AM) shift. Gun towers are located outside of the prison yard and overlook the exercise yards where inmates spend their time when they are not inside a building or their cells. Gun tower officers boarded a van which picked up and dropped off the officers at the start and end of their shift. The van made two runs around the prison, first to drop off the relief officers, and second, to pick up the officers ending their shift.

It was wintertime when this particular devil showed his horns which were aimed to rob, steal, and destroy my peace—his intentions were to break me. I was scheduled for Tower 5, the furthest gun tower from the gatehouse. I was always on time to board the van with the other officers. But this devil, my supervising sergeant who drove the van, wouldn't allow me to board. For six weeks, I was forced to walk to and from the furthest tower enduring the rain, cold, and his sadistic behavior. The other officers couldn't help but notice this injustice yet they did nothing about this abuse. Today we would call that bullying or sexual harassment.

Although none of the other offices did anything to stop the abuse, there was one particular gun tower officer who called me in my tower and told me to pray for this sergeant and love my enemy. I snapped back, "Are you dry, because I am not. Are you boarding the van? I am not. Why don't you pray for him!" She was relentless and eventually this officer got to me. She was like a constant drip of water I couldn't ignore. She asked me if I ever read the Bible and of course I said, "Sure, and I go to church." But in reality, I didn't read the Bible; I only heard bits and pieces of it in church.

Those six weeks of my gun tower duty were agonizing! Not only the long cold walks before and after duty but I also endured this Christian officer who bugged me about reading the Bible and loving my enemies. How could I love someone who didn't even like me?

I picked up a second shift right after my gun tower duty so I could earn double-time money. I was assigned to the MPNC library. The library duty consisted of monitoring the inmates and ensuring their housing units were scheduled for entry. If they were assigned to the library that particular day, their ID would authorize their admission.

As an officer assigned to this detail it was necessary to look at each inmate and match their face to their ID. Believe me, Ms. Rambo didn't care if their mother was dying: if they didn't have the right to be in the library, they certainly were not getting in on my duty. My attitude was, "Go tell your pathetic story to some other officer who had mercy or would break the library rules, not me."

I hated certain types of inmates, inmates who were convicted for child molestation, rape, and murder. I had zero tolerance and I wasn't the only one. Even other inmates had zero tolerance for these criminals. Now I had library duty and was forced to look them in the eye as they approached my library desk.

One particular day, an inmate I despised entered the library. The reason I detested him was because whenever I had responsibility for the night shift prisoner count, this inmate would purposefully masturbate just as I passed his cell. Now here he was and I was supposed to look this animal in the face and give him a moment of my time. I wasn't planning to do that!. When he put his card in my direction, I turned my face to an open book on the librarian's desk and as I looked at it, I realized it was a Bible. A sentence lifted off the pages in bold lettering. I felt compelled to bring it closer in order to reread it. I had never heard this in church, nor had I ever read it in the Bible before or since. The words that jumped off the Bible page that day were, "Wind is the voice of God!"

Wind is the voice of God? Those words were significant to me and even if you can't find those very words in the scripture it doesn't mean I didn't see them. It does mean that the same Holy Spirit which made a donkey talk (Numbers 22:28) spoke to me when no one else could reach me because of my lies and obstinate nature. At that moment, my life changed as the Holy Spirit rerouted my desire to read and study His word.

Those words dug into my soul, because as a little girl from the age of three or four, I hid from my brothers Little Leroy and Chief and found a place where I listened to the wind. I loved hearing the wind whistling through trees and leaves and all of the days of my life I preferred listening to the wind rather than playing with toys, riding bikes, watching sunsets, or partying. Later in life when I became a truck driver, I preferred to drive into the winds of Chicago or a tornado in Kansas than to sit somewhere safe. I loved the wind and now I knew why! When I saw those words, "Wind is the voice of God," they awakened a deep desire to listen to Him rather than anything else in the whole world. I suddenly had a hunger to read His Word, the Bible, so I could hear what He was saying to me.

Later when I returned to Tower 5 duty and that pestering female officer called me in my gun tower, I was waiting for her call with enthusiasm this time. I could truthfully tell her, "I had read the Bible and had a scripture for the next few days to dwell upon: *If your enemy is hungry, feed him; if he is thirsty, give him something to drink; in doing this, you will heap burning coals on his head."* (Romans 12:20 NIV) Loving our enemies is like a burning hot coal to their foreheads! Of course Romans 12:20 isn't speaking of literal burning coals. When we follow Jesus' directions to *"love your enemies, and pray for those who persecute you"* (Matthew 5:44 ESV) and the Biblical instructions *"Do not repay anyone evil for evil"* (Romans 12:17 NIV), it provides a stark contrast. I've heard it explained that to heap "burning coals" is a metaphor for the burning shame someone will feel as their conscience illuminates their contempt-ible behavior.

Being obedient to God's Word meant I had to muster up a way to love someone who didn't like me. It meant I must speak to this sergeant, but speaking wasn't an option as each time I attempted to, he turned his back to me and told those around him he could hear a voice but there was no face and he didn't talk to ghosts! In other words, I didn't exist and he wouldn't acknowledge me.

I had to find another way to love this enemy and since it was Christmas time, I purchased a Christmas card in which I wrote, "God Bless you and Merry Christmas." I selected the timing when I knew he was in the gate-house and handed it to him in the presence of the other officers and his supervisor. They were all aware that he had a problem with me so rather than look foolish in front of the others he accepted it. I think he expected it to be a derogatory note and was taken by surprise. This was my way of loving someone who didn't like me—a simple Christmas card with a "God Bless you and Merry Christmas."

I never saw this sergeant afterward, so his reaction to that Christmas card was a mystery, but I had obeyed the Word of God. The rest was up to Him. Interestingly, God never allowed me to experience that sergeant's wrath again. Within a week, both of his hands closed up like claws, sur-gery was required, but he couldn't drive a van or car and was unable to use a weapon. He was no longer equipped to be even a lowly officer. Due to this unexpected disability, he was forced to take an early retirement.

Later, I ran into this retired sergeant by "accident." Since I don't believe in coincidence, I truthfully don't believe it was an accident. I thought per-haps my Father allowed me to meet this sergeant again as a test. Had I forgiven him? Indeed I had. I truly harbored no bitterness toward him and was genuinely pleased to see him smiling. He owned a corner store and seemed happy and peaceful. It was a delightful change from his previous angry demeanor and I was thrilled for him. I went into that store to buy last-minute treats for my three children, but left with everlasting joy as I witnessed a **"precious moment in hell"** turn into a precious moment for my enemy. Yet another example of what Satan meant for bad, God turned into good for His Glory!

Maybe this story resonates with you? Maybe you have a job situation or an enemy who doesn't even acknowledge you as a person. Maybe there are people who are aware of your difficult circumstances but do nothing to help. I can attest to God's all-powerful ability to comfort you and intercede on your behalf. If God can reach me and lift me from my various circumstances or hells, He can reach into yours as well. What's it going to take? What will be your donkey on the road that talks to you? Here I am! I am trying. Jesus is waiting - He is a simple prayer away.

There were other truly amazing events that occurred while I was a guard at the prison in northern California. One such event took place when I was stationed at the control tower in the center of the prison. This tower was critical as it controlled the flow of physical traffic entering and exiting the prison, from officers coming and going, to inmates (if allowed) entering and exiting to their job sites, doctors' visits, education sites, and so forth. I was told whenever I worked that central tower, *no one*—not even personnel—was allowed in that tower.

When a watch commander called the tower and told me to allow Sgt. Divorce in, I told him that I couldn't unless I was given a direct order. I thought it was a set up, so I immediately went into prayer—the Our Father, the 23rd Psalm. I asked God's Holy Spirit to cover me and take over the situation.

I received the direct order and Sgt. Divorce sat down in my tower. He was unclear as to the reason he'd been sent to my tower; perhaps to relax as he wasn't feeling well. As he spoke, I immediately saw a vision of a wooden chair with no one sitting in it. This sergeant began unburdening his broken heart, crying as he spoke. He disclosed that his wife had filed for divorce, yet they both loved each other. He described how over the past five years he'd raised her now ten year old son and the three of them had been happy. The boy was very smart: an A student who could take a radio apart and put it back together! But the son had stopped listening to anyone, had become a troubled child and his grades declined. The problems with the stepson had led to stress in the marriage and his wife saw no way out but divorce.

The wooden chair in my vision now had a little boy in it and Jesus was standing behind the chair and little boy. I wondered how much I should share with this Sergeant about my God given gift of visions. I had asked God to take control over our meeting in this tower so I needed to trust Him. I thought, "Yes, there is a chance that Sgt. Divorce will think I am loony, but he also might be willing to pray with me and receive the meaning of the vision." So I boldly shared the vision God had shown me.

I asked him if he would pray with me and allow God to give us His meaning to this vision. Sgt. Divorce told me he was a Christian and believed in spiritual gifts even though he didn't think he had any. I said, "Sgt. Divorce, I see the Lord standing behind a wooden chair with a little boy sitting in it." The sergeant asked me to describe the little boy. It definitely fit his stepson's description. Then, I said, "The Lord has His hands over the boy's ears."

Sgt. Divorce said, "That is exactly his problem. He won't listen to me anymore. His mother and I agree on that problem."

I asked, "Have you had his ears checked?"

He said they had been to every kind of doctor, therapist, and counselor. However, he wasn't sure if he had been to an ENT.

This miserable, brokenhearted man scheduled an appointment and took his son to an audiologist. They learned that the boy, who once could hear, had lost his ability to hear. His grades had dropped because he couldn't express his hearing problem and was unable to select a front row seat in his classroom where he could hear better or read the teacher's lips. Discovering the reason for his stepson's behavioral changes was the first step. It provided an opportunity for them to work together for a better future. The husband and wife were reconciled and she dropped the divorce proceedings.

This family's hellish situation, disclosed in the prison control tower, was answered by God's intervention as He set them free from their hell - another **precious moment!**

WORKPLACE PERSECUTION

"Blessed are you when they revile and persecute you, and say all kinds of evil against you falsely for My sake."

MATTHEW 5:11 NKJV

"Once upon a time"—a familiar start to a story. This once upon a time picks up when I was an injured truck driver working for Winners Circle out of Southgate, California. As an injured worker, I was offered an indoor job for a season while my injury healed.

A few details prior to the injury; I would drove in the snow, rain, mountains, as well as Los Angeles traffic and it didn't bother me. Yet, whenever I pulled over at a border crossing, parked my rig, and submitted my log and paperwork to the highway patrol, I was suddenly nerve-racked. Why did I get nervous? Because I was not completely confident that I was one hundred percent correct with every minute logged, that my tandems were at the correct measurements, or that my truck and trailer would pass an inspection. I understood my job was on the line as the responsible party tasked with getting my load to a destination in a precise time slot. Time was of the utmost importance as a truck driver. I often said, "We hurry up and wait." That was part of the job and every day was a challenge, more so for a woman, as in any male dominated occupation.

There was a sense of personal pride when I, a little woman, parked my big rig right beside the big boys, got out of the truck, strutted to wherever I needed to be, and attended to the business at hand. I loved the daily sense of accomplishments and the feeling of a well-deserved pat on the back. My injury somehow tarnished that sense of pride. I was both physically and emotionally injured. Being a woman in a man's world, I suddenly felt like the weaker vessel.

My injury was a severely pulled lower back muscle, sustained when trying to unlock a jammed tandem. The tandem was part of my 53-foot trailer. I was resetting the wheels to adjust the load, correcting the weight on the border scales, otherwise, I could not proceed. Unable to drive due to this injury, my company had to get a replacement driver and I flew back to California.

What Satan meant for bad, God turned into an opportunity for me to shine inside an office setting as I worked and earned an income while healing. I met a wonderful man who became a dear friend. He worked as a safety instructor for Winners Circle. Pastor Art was a Christian and we hit it off almost instantly. We could shuck and jive as truck drivers do, but also toss around Christian language with ease. As long as we didn't mention the name Jesus or Bible studies inside the office, it was acceptable. For example, "If He is for us, who can be against us?" Only someone familiar with the Bible would even recognize that as a Bible verse. All day long Pastor Art and I threw those verses in the air as we sowed seeds. People heard the Word of the Lord and we knew His word never comes back void!

I worked in the supply room and made life a little easier and more organized for the safety instructors and other office staff. It normally took the safety instructors several hours to get organized and ready for weekly classes of 50 to 100 new truck drivers. I relieved them of these classroom preparations. All they had to do was teach and not fret over their equipment or books and updated folders. They loved the idea of walking to a shelf and picking up their ready-made folders. Computers on the desks were in their right settings and turned on for their truck drivers. Many truck drivers had never sat in a classroom or ever used a computer but a week of safety training was a requirement at Winners Circle. I understood the value of training on road safety and the transportation industry regulations.

While sitting in the supply room, I had lots of moments to ask God, "Why am I sitting in the closet?" "Why did you allow me to get injured?" "What is it you want me to learn, Lord, or did you save my life from a truck fatality?" "I don't understand you Lord, but I trust you." I often said, "I don't know what tomorrow holds, but I know who holds my tomorrows!"

There I was working in a supply room and making friends inside the Safety office. The instructors all liked me except one female in the office. She hated me and told lies about me. Whenever I asked a simple question, she cut me off. Whenever she did that, the other office staff looked in my direction with an embarrassed sort of expression. Somehow, that validated it wasn't just my imagination. She humiliated me more than once and she loved to do it in front of an audience. Fortunately, the supply room was a safe place to hide whenever her horns showed. I spent a lot of time praying while I was in that supply room.

Again other people didn't do anything about the bully in the office. Rather, they pretended to not hear her, but they knew as well as I did that her behavior was wrong. In those instances the words I had heard so long ago echoed in my mind, "they will treat you the same way they treated your Father." The Bible says, *If it is possible on your part, live at peace with everyone. "Do not avenge yourselves, beloved, but leave room for God's wrath. For it is written: "Vengeance is Mine; I will repay, says the Lord."* (Romans 12:18–19 NIV)

Thankfully she was the only person at Winners Circle who didn't like me and was bent on humiliating me. She seemed obsessed with getting me fired but the tables were turned when she made a huge mistake. She posted a racial and age discrimination cartoon. She ultimately was the one terminated.

In the meantime, I healed and went back to driving my truck. Pastor

Art and I remained good friends. I saw him at the office whenever I returned for training and we often got together during my time off. One day after parking my truck I went into the office. He met me with a smile and asked me if I would ever consider becoming a safety instructor. He thought I was good with the truck drivers, knew the office procedures, and seemed to fit right in. I asked, "What does it pay?" He said the magic words. I responded, "Of course, if God opens that door, I would love to be a safety instructor."

When the position opened up Pastor Art put in a good word for me. His word was gold at Winners Circle Southgate headquarters. I prayed about it and everything worked out. I walked right into the job. I was a safety instructor nearly three years when a new sheriff came to town, I mean a new safety manager. It didn't take long and her dislike for me was evident. Why do I bring that out in certain women? Perhaps it is God's spirit in me they are rejecting? I don't know. I treat everyone the same and I have been great at any career I have ever undertaken. It was obvious to the other instructors that she would pick on me. When they would interject on my behalf, she would shut them up. She didn't want to hear it.

Providentially, every time she thought she had tripped me up, I had the answers. This seemed to enrage her more. Finally the staff asked, "What did you do to her to make her hate you?" I didn't have a clue. I didn't know her any better than the rest of them. But I did know that I Peter 5:8 ESV tells us, *"Be sober-minded; be watchful. Your adversary the devil prowls around like a roaring lion, seeking someone to devour."* I could see the signs of a setup, and the Lord revealed to me to watch my back and pay close attention to Him.

I reinjured my back in the supply room and had to take six weeks off. I took advantage of the time off from this wicked woman and made sure my Worker's Comp injury was legal and that all my i's were dotted and t's were crossed. I suspected she was scheming to get me fired.

I had visited a Worker's Comp attorney to be sure of my rights knowing the Holy Spirit doesn't warn me of things unless it's going to happen and I needed to walk in confidence, not in fear. After all God's Word says, *"For God has not given us a spirit of fear, but of power and of love and of a sound mind."* (2 Timothy 1:7 NKJV)

I had given her a week notice of the day the doctor said I could return to work. The day my Worker's Comp leave ended, she was waiting for me with human resources. I was prepared.

I heard her husband was ill and taking a turn for the worse. The Holy Spirit was nudging me to pray for him and ask God to take away his illness as a sign. The Lord has promised to hear and answer our prayers. *"Call to Me and I will answer you...."* (Jeremiah 33:3 NKJV). I also knew that what Satan means for harm (anything and everything), God can turn around for His glory if we have faith the size of a mustard seed.

So there I sat at her desk as she terminated me. She said I was a day late returning to work and they no longer needed me. She asked if I had any questions. I said, "No, but may I make a comment?"

She said "Sure."

I stood up as the human resources person was standing and I said, "I just need to pray right now. Do you mind?" They looked at each other, shrugged their shoulders, and allowed me to pray. I prayed for her sick husband and asked God to heal him and allow this moment to be a sign that He hears me and I also asked God's will to be done in my life. Amen! I excused myself to call my attorney and let him take it from there.

I was unlawfully terminated and am not allowed to disclose what the winning resolution was but I can say God was faithful. In addition to my positive resolution, the husband received immediate healing. God is good!

"If God is for us who can be against us?" (Romans 8:31 NIV) Another **precious moment in hell!**

From Addiction to Abundance

"For as he thinks in his heart, so is he."

PROVERBS 23:7 NKJV

This scripture, *"For as he thinks in his heart, so is he..."* (Proverbs 23:7 NKJV) is one of God's truths. My outlook was greatly impacted by the nun/angel's precious words given to me the day my tragic foster care life began. Those words were hidden in my heart and every time they came to my mind, they helped me endure the difficulties, knowing that Jesus had gone before me. The Bible says, *"The LORD Himself goes before you; He will be with you. He will never leave you or forsake you. Do not be afraid or discouraged."* (Deuteronomy 31:8 NIV)

The nun/angel didn't tell me to share those words with my brothers and it never occurred to me to do so. My brothers didn't receive those encouraging words, and their life perspective was much different from mine. I don't know why I never shared that angel story with my brothers but I wish I had thought to do so earlier. When my brother, Little Leroy, was on his deathbed, I finally told him about it.

My brothers and I faced many challenges over the years and through the valleys we walked. We each coped with our pain, sorrow, and loneliness in different ways. My brothers sought to mask theirs, succumbing to heroin and other drug addictions. I could have easily become a participant, but I saw how their addictions hurt people along their paths and how it destroyed their families. My mother and brothers traveled a similar road; it was not the direction that I wanted for my life. Why would I choose to travel into their valley of brokenness? Yes, they needed a way to deal with their painful experiences but their choices weren't working out so well for them. I chose to deal with my pain by applying what I had learned from the Bible, allowing myself to be wrapped securely in the loving arms of Jesus. Deuteronomy 33:27 NIV says, *"The eternal God is your refuge, and underneath are the everlasting arms...."* It wasn't until much later that my brothers learned to treat their pain with a proven remedy. They gave their pain over to our great healer, our loving and forgiving God, our everlasting Father; and they finally experienced peace! Little LeRoy felt overwhelming joy, faith and an abundance of hope. Chief began living in peace, faith and forgiveness. They no longer had cravings for different forms of sedation because they found their peace in Jesus, just like our mother did when she accepted Jesus into her heart. Who the Son sets free, is free indeed! They experienced what Psalm 23:5 describes as "my cup runneth over" because their cups (hearts) were overflowing with love, joy, peace, and hope!

Because we live in a fallen world, this life frequently has its troubles and sufferings, some of which I've heard referred to as hell on earth. But God knows our suffering, He suffered too. The Bible tells of Jesus' birth and how Herod searched for the infant with the intent of having Him killed. His parents, being warned by an angel, fled to a foreign land, so obviously life must have been hard for them. Here on earth many of God's children suffer in many ways at every age. This journey called life can be a hard road. Jesus said, *"In this world you will have trouble, but take heart, I have overcome the world."* (John 16:33b NIV). The apostle Paul wrote, *"Yet what we suffer now is nothing compared to the glory He will reveal to us later."* (Romans 8:18 NLT) So for His name's sake, I share my experiences of **precious moments in hell** so that others might know there is hope! Jesus did all the hard work and He said on the cross, "It is finished!" All we have to do is believe and accept Jesus as our Lord and Savior, turn away from our sin and give it to Him, in return we are promised an eternal life with no more pain and suffering – the reward Jesus earned for us on that cross! *"He will wipe away every tear from their eyes, and there will be no more death or mourning or crying or pain, for the former things have passed away."* (Revelation 21:4 NKJV)

How comforting to know that God's hand in heaven is reaching down to us, He feels our pain, and He has a plan for a future without pain! The Word says He bottles every tear and knows the count of hairs on our heads. Think about that—how amazing that he knows us so intimately. Not only that, but in Hebrews 13:5 He promised, "I will never leave you nor forsake you." I am blessed, I am cared for by someone who will never leave me or forsake me, and so are you! No, it's not easy, no it doesn't end all the challenges. No, I don't have all the answers why He allows bad things to happen. But I do know I was able to survive my childhood because Jesus was with me, that His eyes were upon me constantly, without taking a rest. This is my testimony and encouragement; we can be certain that He will be with us to help us through all the mountains and valleys, the challenges which are set before us.

I do not recommend for anyone to travel alone in the valleys of life and neither does my Father. He said, *"Two are better than one, because they have a good reward for their toil. For if they fall, one will lift up his fellow. But woe to him who is alone when he falls and has not another to lift him up!"* (Ecclesiastes 4:9–10 ESV) I have been in caves and crevices, dark places where only God could see me. It certainly was not a good place to be. However, because I allowed God to help me in the dark places of my life, He shed light on my path and I was able to escape. I learned many lessons in those hard places. Later there were times when I tried to caution my brothers and my children to step away from a cliff where they were teetering on its edge, but they chose to ignore my words of advice and toppled into the pit. Other times they were enticed by an alluring cave despite my warning. It looked appealing on the outside, but on the inside it was indeed that same scary cave that I had advised them to avoid. God said "woe to him who is alone when he falls." Sometimes my brothers and my children chose to walk alone, entering their dark caves, refusing to call on God for help. I had to stand by and watch; it was painful but I was powerless to help and as much as I wanted to be, I came to realize I was not their shepherd. I could not provide the protection and guidance needed like our Good Shepherd provides for us. Life can definitely be easier if we have another to help lift us up, but the truth is, we may not always be able to depend on another human being, sometimes they are simply unavailable or unable to help, but Jesus never lets us down. He is always there for us! Each person must choose for him or herself. Will you choose Jesus? The Bible says, *"Choose for yourselves this day whom you will serve...."* (Joshua 24:15 NKJV). I am glad I can say like Joshua, *"As for me and my house, we will serve the LORD."* (Joshua 24:15 NKJV)

While I am confident that God's plan is for good and that He will see us through our challenges, I also know God's timing is not always our timing. The apostle Peter wrote, *"But do not overlook this one fact, beloved, that with the Lord one day is as a thousand years, and a thousand years as one day."* (2 Peter 3:8 ESV) This means sometimes it takes patience as we wait on the Lord. I assure you the wait is worth it—I have experienced the blessings at the end of the wait.

Some Want Magic,
I Prefer Miracles!

"Jesus performed many other signs in the presence of his disciples, which are not recorded in this book. But these are written that you may believe that Jesus is the Messiah, the Son of God, and that by believing you may have life in his name."

JOHN 20:30–31 NIV

I am not the Almighty Miracle Worker, but I am one He sometimes uses when something phenomenal is about to happen and He wants someone to act at the drop of a hat. God has placed thoughts in my mind, taken over my dream state, and warned me when my life was in danger. He has sent me into fields where I stuck out like a sore thumb. I have been called into storms, yet with the storm comes a rainbow and when He is finished using me in a specific arena, I can always look back at the miracle that was at the end of the rainbow!

We needed a miracle when we were children. Remember God's timing and that He can turn what Satan meant for evil and use it for good—well, I believe my brothers and I are the miracle as are many others who have endured childhood trauma, courtroom trauma, and war trauma. We are a witness that you can walk out of the shadows of darkness if you surrender to your Maker. This is exactly what I did when I prayed for my brothers and their predicaments.

My brother, Little Leroy, was only five years old when he was used to unknowingly commit a crime. His bad actions seemed to spiral downward from there until he faced prison in his late teens. My brother Chief headed in the same direction. Both were housed in the Santa Clara/San Jose criminal system awaiting their sentencing hearings. Both were looking at a five-year-to-life sentence for their crimes. They had the same history and did their crimes together, therefore, they each attended the other's hearing; shackled with chains around their waists and ankles, hands cuffed and each in an orange jumpsuit.

I didn't realize that my brothers were on a crime spree until I got a call from their public defender while I was working as the San Joaquin County administrator intern. It is the head position of a county seat governing the Board of Supervisors. I am sure my position seemed impressive to my brothers and their public defender. At that time I didn't know much about politics, but learned quickly how to identify those who really control the county and how quickly a law could be changed to fit the mood of the people who are elected officials. It was a learning position that I knew I could use later in life but for sure this seat gave me clout for my brothers' sentencing hearing. The letterhead was golden bullets for the prosecutor's desk and the judge. In other words, they thought I was somebody to listen to.

I lived in the rural town of San Joaquin, California. San Jose was several hours away by car. I didn't want to take time out of my life from college and my new job so I decided I would pray and see what God wanted me to do. I was on my knees, lifting my hands to His majesty hoping I would be heard. I started crying for my two brothers and asking, "Why did they have to experience so much madness when I knew they had good, loving hearts?"

Yes, we reap what we sow, and they both had heroin habits and with that comes thievery which they had repeated for several years in several counties and now it was time to pay: five to life! The public defender thought if I gave a mercy plea, the judge would reduce the sentence from life in prison. While I was pleading my heart out to God, I woke up on my front room floor in a cross position as if I had been nailed to a cross lying on my floor. I had placed my life at the feet of Jesus Christ and, although I didn't know at the time but what happened to me is known by some as being slain in the spirit. I knew when I got up from my living room floor that I would indeed travel to San Jose and give a speech on behalf of my brothers. If I'd had a magic wand, I would have waved it and set them free. I desperately hoped they would be given another chance to change their wretched hellish lives. But a magic wand is a fairytale: they needed a real-life miracle. I am no miracle worker, but I know one!

It was bad enough that while they committed their crimes of theft within the community of retirees, an elderly woman bit my brother while he attempted to escape through her bedroom window. His blood trail is what led the police to their capture. She tried holding on to his hand as she dialed 9-1-1. The incident made the news: "An 80-year-old lady captures thief with her teeth." That sounds like a good headline, right? But it's pretty embarrassing for an inmate when you're taken down by an old lady and just her teeth. Sad, but true. Well, let's get to the miracle.

I sat in the witness chair, swore to tell the truth, the whole truth and nothing but the truth. The judge gave me the opportunity to give a mercy plea for my brothers who sat shackled together. I told the story of our childhood in the foster home. I told of our first seven years: daily torture beatings with leather belts while we bent over a bathtub wearing nothing but our underwear; the times I had to watch thread tied around their private parts or a rubber band tightened around their private parts; the times we stood on the edge of our street with urine-stained sheets over our heads; and the times my brothers were tied to anthills. We were rescued seven years later when I dressed out for P.E. in junior high and my P.E. teacher saw the belt welts new and old. The school nurse and authorities discovered my brothers had the same belt welts.

While I was being recorded, the court reporter was in tears; the courtroom was hushed. The public defender or prosecutor did not interrupt, but was also in distress as were others in suits sitting in the court proceedings. We were all pretty much in tears, yet my plea was surrendering to the court and perhaps this moment was planned before my brothers and I knew it would take place. Perhaps I was given the county administration position for such a time as this.

We had always been at the mercy of the court system even as children and now we faced the court system as young adults. After I made my mercy plea, I was not excused from my witness seat and had to remain near the judge. The judge told my brothers to stand up as he called them by name, "Mr. Leroy Yanez and Mr. Chief Yanez, you both face five to life today: I hereby sentence both of you to ninety days, with time served." In other words, both my brothers walked out of their circumstances within a week of this hearing. Now if that wasn't a miracle, I don't know what is. Perhaps the most Almighty Miracle Worker is the one who creates those He uses in His miracle works? I'm not sure who is more blessed: the one who receives the miracle or the one He chooses to use in the miracle? All I know is my brothers and I were grateful for that miracle!

The judge also believed that the Army would be a good place for both of them as the Vietnam War was underway. They both gladly took the deal and joined the military.

There were other miracles which no mere magician could perform, such as bringing the dead back to life and saving a terminally ill person who was only breaths away from passing from this life to another. God chose me as a witness and catalyst for just such an undertaking.

While managing security at a large hospital in Long Beach, I had the full responsibility of the hospital's flow of traffic—staff, visitors, doctors, nurses, police, paramedics, ambulance, and dispatch. Therefore, whenever a trauma was being received in ER, especially gunshot victims, we went on high alert to protect the medical premises and everything on board. High alert was necessary as a precaution in case the gunshot victim was a gang member and other gang members and/or their rivals showed up at the hospital. One particular night our dispatch was on high alert as well as all our security staff. We received a call from local sheriff and EMT that we had a DOA (Dead on Arrival) in route.

I clearly heard a voice tell me to meet the DOA and plead the Blood of Jesus on him. "What? Not me … I can't do that while I am in uniform and head of security, Lord. Take this cup from me!" Then I heard that same voice tell me to find the victim's family in ER and tell them he would be all right! "Seriously? Not me Lord. He is DOA!"

Again I was told to go plead the Blood of Jesus on this victim and I knew the authoritative voice of the Supreme Commander as I had heard it many times before. So I walked into ER where police, doctors, and nurses were cutting this victim's clothes off and doing everything they could to revive him. I walked to his head where he had been shot and said, "I plead the Blood of Jesus on you." No one in that small room seemed to see me much less hear me. Having obeyed, I walked out. Then I heard that same Supreme Voice tell me to go tell his family he was going to be all right.

I was thinking to myself, "tomorrow is my day off and I don't want to suffer the consequences for praying for someone while on duty and also telling someone their dead family member was going to be all right!" But the Almighty Miracle Worker wouldn't leave me alone until I surrendered. I walked into the visiting area of ER and asked if there were any family members who were here for the gunshot victim. This little African-American grandmother stood up and we met each other. I got real close to her face and asked her if she was a praying woman. She said, "Yes, I am."

I said, "Do you believe if we have the faith of a mustard seed we can move mighty mountains in Jesus' name?"

She said, "Yes, I do."

I said, "Do you believe if we are in agreement on anything on earth that it will be established in heaven?"

She said, "Yes, I do."

I said, "Would you like to pray with me?"

She said, "Yes."

I led us in prayer in that visiting room as we held each other's hands. After we said, "Amen," I told her the Lord said, "He is going to be all right!" My mission was complete. I did what the Creator told me to do. The rest was up to Him and even when we are faithless, He is faithful.

I didn't stick around to see if he was all right. He had been shot in the head by his ex-wife, not by gang members, so our high alert was no longer high, yet still on alert in the event that the shooter attempted to finish the job.

Truthfully speaking, I never know how or why God uses me, but I am sure He can do all things and He is far greater than any mere magician.

When my two days of off duty were over and I returned to work, I asked if anything was new and did I need to be brushed up on any events? First thing was the outcome of the shooting victim and the call that dispatch received regarding the praying guard which she knew had to be me. The dispatcher was my friend and so were many of the security staff because I took care of them and they took care of me. She said, "The grandmother asked for you to visit her and her grandson when you came in."

I said, "What happened? Is he in our morgue?"

"No, he lived and is in our rehab unit."

The bullet lodged in his head. He has to learn to walk and talk again, but "he is all right."

Now, what might have happened if I hadn't obeyed the mighty Creator? He nudged me to use my favorite prayer, "I plead the Blood of Jesus on you," and He told me to tell the family member the DOA would be all right. Actually, I used prayer to reach out to God through this woman, because the Bible tells us when two or more are gathered in His name, He is right there in the midst of us! *"For where two or three are gathered together in my name, there am I in the midst of them."* (Matthew 18:20 KJV) He honored that obedience and those prayers! I stand on His word, which never comes back void. Amen!

One last story of a miracle work. This is my last powerful story originating out of the large hospital in Long Beach. Veronica opened the door to my job at this hospital. If it wasn't for her leading, I would never have considered working for a hospital. Thank you, Veronica, wherever you are, as God used you to set up His works through me. Some people like to call it magic but I know better. This last story was astounding! I did indeed walk through the shadows of death yet came out smelling like a rose with another **"precious moment in hell"** to tell.

The large hospital in Long Beach is impeccable when it comes to its care and safety of their children and all measures are taken to keep anyone from entering the children's area unless they are meant to be there. This next miracle took place while I was interim manager for their security. We were on alert for an influx of potential off-schedule visitation for a child who was not expected to live another day. That situation allowed anyone who knew the child to have a last-minute visit. The children's ward has multiple cameras scanning from dispatch plus foot patrol throughout all shifts, especially nights.

It was around 9:00 PM and we noticed an African-American gang enter the children's ward. They were known as the "Bloods" and were wearing their color scarves portraying what gang they represented. They had to go through our visiting area to get a visitor badge and acknowledge who they were visiting. It happened to be the father of the dying child, so we couldn't say no to that admission. Once I acknowledged their legitimate visitation and allowed the three of them upstairs, I clearly heard a voice tell me to approach the father and ask him, "Would you do anything to save your son's life?"

One might think after all the profound experiences God has given me that it would be easy to obey. Not so! I thought to myself, "Yea, right, I am going to approach this gang member with my security badge outfit and ask him that question. I don't think so." But again I have learned the voice of the Creator and when He tells me to do something He tells me over and over again until I can think of nothing else except what He has on His agenda. So it took three times for me to hear that still small voice and knew I wouldn't be able to concentrate on the rest of my duties until I was obedient. Therefore, I asked the young man if I could speak to him alone and he said, "Why and heck, no! And I have a right to be here. That's my son in there dying."

I asked again, "Please, sir, may I pray with you?"

Another "Heck no! That woman over there is my kid's mother. She does all that crap!" So now we were making a scene in a very soft stage, the dying son's room was glass and I could see he looked like he was around seven years old, frail, and almost lifeless. His separated wife, grandmother, pastor, and others who were there for this crucial moment approached me and asked if they could be of any help. I said, "Yes, the Lord wants me to ask this father if he will do anything to save his son's life?"

They were all in agreement and it felt as if God had called me to their prayer group. They saw me as an opportunity to get this child's father involved. They looked at him and said, "You need to listen to this woman who has a message from the Lord. Whether you believe or not, you can answer her question."

He surrendered to their pressure and told me to go ahead and ask. I said, "Sir, the Lord wants to know if you would do anything to save your son's life?" That's all.

He said, "Yes, but not in such nice terminology." In retrospect, I think he used the inappropriate language as a way to feel tough while surrendering. After he said, "Yes," then the Lord told me what he needed to do—now this moment was taking place as this group of people were praying and praising God.

I said, "Sir, the Lord wants you to go in your son's room and plead the Blood of Jesus on him three times while your hand hovers over his chest."

He didn't have a clue what I was saying as if he never used the word "Jesus" before. But he had the ex-wife write the words down so he would remember what to say, and had me repeat what he was to do. I did. Then I left. I didn't want to be there and see the results in person. Besides, this was my Friday and I would be home for two days after this shift ended.

I knew I was going to be in trouble with the security director, who already didn't like me, because his best friend and the sergeant of the hospital security was terminated when I brought charges of sexual discrimination against one of my female officers. His unwanted advances continued and it was on camera and audible. He didn't have any recourse as sexual discrimination was not tolerated. The director had to terminate him. Retaliation was also not tolerated and yet it seemed my head was on the chopping block.

Remember I said there were cameras everywhere in the hospital, so when I held hands with this family and bowed my head to pray it was on tape and I was in hot water. But so be it, I was obeying the Almighty Creator.

Wouldn't you know, the director called me on Sunday and told me to arrive one hour early for my shift on Monday and to meet him in the main lobby. I thought, "Here it comes, my walking papers in a non-hostile environment."

I arrived early as expected but called my friend, Bob B, in security first. He wouldn't tell me anything except the lobby was full of people. This was before visiting hours, so there shouldn't have been a crowd in the lobby. I didn't know what to expect but I was expecting the worst.

When I walked through the lobby doors, I saw my boss in the far back waiting for me. Truthfully he didn't actually want to see me. I was there for the crowd who was waiting for me. It was the same crowd who I had prayed with on Friday night. They had flowers, balloons, and they were lit up like candles. They had a surprise for me. They slowly opened up the crowd which was surrounding a wheelchair. It was the little boy who received a miracle that night and was on his way home! Wow! That was so incredible. I am blown away by what the Almighty Creator can do! All things are possible!

But that wasn't all of it. They said, "No, we have more! Wait for it!" They opened the crowd further and behind the pastor stood three men in suits and ties. It was the little boy's father and his two ex-gang members! The three of them witnessed a miracle and then became yet another miracle, three souls saved from Hell and the **precious moment** where God interceded on their behalf and for His name's sake!

BROKEN BEFORE VIETNAM, SHATTERED AFTER

"'If you can?' said Jesus. 'Everything is possible for one who believes.' Immediately the boy's father exclaimed, 'I do believe; help me overcome my unbelief!'"

MARK 9:23–24 NIV

H is whole life he had survived the pain of being placed in unsafe and abusive situations through no fault of his own. His name was Little Leroy, my little brother.

Both of our parents were from a small farm town and neither were integrated into any Christian culture. Basically their physical desire was their god. They followed the rule, "Thou shall get whatever you can and to hell with the consequences or the damage caused!" Our mother used to say, "What you see is what you get," and "If you don't like my peaches, don't shake my tree!" My father's approach was, "I am the man of the family and what I say goes! If I need to drink, drive, and be merry, I will with whoever I want, whenever I want because I am the man!"

Needless to say, this was not a cozy, loving, family environment; it was survival of the fittest. A life of manipulation and self-absorption passed on from parent to child through observation. Little Leroy became a survivor while he was still in diapers; yet as he grew older he became tired and weary. By the time he went to Vietnam he was already wounded, scarred, and at the edge of hopelessness.

Because of his dysfunctional family life with parents who did not want or care for his siblings or him, Little Leroy developed a chronic expectancy of being a target for pain. With no one but me to wrap their arms around him from the age of three to fifteen, it just wasn't enough. He grew increasingly vacant within his heart and mind.

From outward appearances, no one would have ever known about his internal pain. He had a knack for making people laugh—that good deep belly kind of laugh. He was always a joy to be around. He also consistently stood up for the underdog. He was your best friend and literally would take a bullet for you. No one dared speak ill of someone he cared about because he would quickly tell them, "Shut up or I will shut you up." And he meant it! I have seen him shut a few people up and it was a quick—one, two—and they were picking themselves up from the floor. He didn't care if the person you were speaking about was a total jerk. He didn't want to hear you speak disparagingly of anyone, especially behind their back.

You learned quickly who Little Leroy was; first he was quiet, handsome, energetic, loved to play poker, loved women, made you laugh, and was solid as a rock as far as being your brother or friend. Little Leroy was the man you could count on to give you the shirt off his back, even his shoes; I witnessed that too. Little Leroy walked home in his socks more than once because he thought someone else deserved shoes. He did it because that someone else was loved by someone, somewhere, but mainly because that someone wanted to live. Most of Little Leroy's life he didn't want to live. From the age of ten, He started asking God to let him die. So Little Leroy struggled with a death wish for years. You might, too, if you were being raised in a foster home only 36 miles away from your biological parents who didn't come to visit, the foster care mom was physically abusing and tormenting your siblings and you, you had nowhere to lay your head for a moment of peace, your guts hurt when you woke up each morning not because of the bad food but because of the daily whippings you knew were coming.

Life had been torturously harsh. Early on, every time he and his brother got a haircut, they didn't know if the razor blade was for their neck or their hair. Even the buzz haircut hurt. Why did Little Leroy and Chief have to get a buzz haircut when other boys in the foster home were allowed to grow their hair? That's what Mr. H was directed to give them. Whatever Mrs. H. told him to do, he did. For seven years both Little Leroy and Chief were cursed with a buzz haircut. After their first few years of Dad cutting their hair, they didn't fear he would cut them with the razor anymore. Dad wasn't the torturer—that was Mom.

Little Leroy seemed to be the brave one when it came to walking in the dark and standing up for the first blow. He couldn't stand to hear any-one cry. As young as he was and as timid as he seemed, he would always help the underdog even when he was a toddler.

I can remember when Chief was told to go out in the dark for any reason: feed the dogs, empty the trash, shut the back door in the garage or whatever. He didn't want to go alone. As long as Little Leroy went with him, he wasn't as afraid. That carried over to their high school years as well. Whenever Chief instigated a fight after school, it would be Little Leroy who was there to defend him. He had Chief or me carry his books while he handled the matter and Little Leroy was always the winner.

Many a school day, you could hear the rumble in the halls, "There is a fight after school!"

"Who?"

"The Yanez brothers and…!"

Fighting actually started in the H home. Mrs. H would force Chief and Little Leroy to hit each other and if they didn't she would hit them with the leather strap. I don't know why. We didn't know why she did many of the unimaginable things she did. The cruelty seemed to have no bounds. It was inconceivable that someone charged with the care of three young children by Social Services would treat them with such cruelty. I was forced to watch unspeakable tortures inflicted on my baby brothers. If I dropped a tear, all three of us got whipped.

Additionally, her eldest son, Carrot Top, seemed to have a mean streak. He reveled watching Chief and Little Leroy cry or squirm. Many times Carrot Top sat on their faces and farted; or rubbed his underarm pits in their noses. Mrs. H and Carrot Top inflicted permanent emotional damage on those two little boys.

Understanding our circumstances was inconceivable at the time when we were busy surviving. So in order to survive, Little Leroy learned to swallow the tears and act as if those painful events were not happening to him. But you can be sure he became calloused as a little boy and later was a broken and hardened young man. Somehow, he could still make you laugh in the midst of afflictions. He managed to lighten the atmosphere and give a bit of cheer even in the tough times.

Little Leroy liked to sing. When we walked to the school bus stop, he would sing little songs like, "Down by the Billabong," "Davey Crocket," and "Row, Row, Row Your Boat." He would only sing "Jesus Loves Me" if we were alone, because every time we did we would cry, and Little Leroy never wanted anyone to see him cry. He loved Jesus but as he grew increasingly despondent, Jesus was pushed into the background of his life, because his thoughts were, "How can Jesus love me and allow all these bad things to happen?" Many of us face similar thoughts and doubts sometimes. God understands; it is human to experience doubts. This must be the reason there are Bible verses that deal with doubt. One that is particularly encouraging is *"Lord, I believe; help my unbelief!"* (Mark 9:24 NKJV) Even Thomas, one of the twelve disciples, had doubts after Jesus had died and he was told of His resurrection. The other disciples were present when Jesus first appeared after his resurrection but Thomas was not there. He missed it and refused to believe, *"So the other disciples told him, 'We have seen the Lord!' But he said to them, 'Unless I see the nail marks in his hands and put my finger where the nails were, and put my hand into his side, I will not believe.'"* (John 20:25 NIV) Jesus himself came to Thomas and compassionately addressed Thomas's doubts, *"Then he said to Thomas, 'Put your finger here; see my hands. Reach out your hand and put it into my side. Stop doubting and believe.' Thomas said to him, My Lord and my God!"* (John 20:27–28 NIV) Unfortunately, the pain clouded Little Leroy's eyes and the questioning doubts seemed to happen to Little Leroy all his life—especially in Vietnam.

As Little Leroy became a young man, it was important to him that people knew he didn't say or admit to something he wasn't sure of. Whatever Little Leroy said you could take to the bank. You certainly were not going to win an argument he was sure of. It was best to just shut up and not make him smoke a whole pack of cigarettes or wager you that he was right. He did like to gamble and you would likely lose.

One night he saw a bearskin at a poker game and he wanted it badly. He wanted to win it for me and didn't quit the game until he had it in his arms. He was so proud of that bearskin and wanted me to know how much he appreciated me when he was in Vietnam. I was the only person who wrote to him while he was in the midst of war. It was a terrible shame that even though his parents were older and should have been wiser, they still didn't write him a letter. More pain.

Why would he expect love from our parents when they had turned their backs on the first children they brought into this world? I suppose no matter how old we get, we still desire love from our parents no matter what they have done in our past. I believe this desire for love has been instilled in our hearts by our Father, God. And He alone extends unconditional love that we cannot be separated from! *"Who shall separate us from the love of Christ? Shall trouble or hardship or persecution or famine or nakedness or danger or sword... For I am convinced that neither death nor life, neither angels nor demons, neither the present nor the future, nor any powers, neither height nor depth, nor anything else in all creation, will be able to separate us from the love of God that is in Christ Jesus our Lord.* (Romans 8:35, 38-39 NIV)

Even though our parents seemed incapable of loving us, Little Leroy loved them. But in the depth of his soul he couldn't forgive them for not loving us and caring for us. He was always in emotional and mental pain and turned to drugs and booze to drown his sorrow. His drug addiction didn't stop him from functioning in the Vietnam jungle—he survived that hell too. I remember him telling me when he got back from Vietnam he wished I could see the monkey on his back. I always thought he had a pet monkey riding on his shoulder, tipping him off to the enemy. I didn't know the monkey on his back was really a drug that killed the pain and nearly killed him. It certainly killed his relationships with his children until later in life.

I would have never believed my brothers were hooked on such drugs. Why would they go there? I'm certain some so-called "friend" gave them their first fix free. Once they were hooked, the friend had a constant buyer. Friends like this we do not need! Oh, that my brothers had known, *"Do not be misled: "Bad company corrupts good charac-ter."* (1 Corinthians 15:33 NIV)

After sustaining a shrapnel wound on Little Leroy's first tour in Vietnam, the Army bandaged him up and sent him home. Little Leroy came home in one piece physically but mentally he was shattered. He came home with more pain, broken in more ways than one. He had PTSD and he had a need for more drugs to "hide the real hard stuff," he would say.

To make matters worse, on his way home from Vietnam, he flew into San Diego where a friend picked him up. On his way home, the car he was riding in was hit head on and Little Leroy went through the wind-shield. I know by the Grace of God Little Leroy survived but surely you can understand that he felt like a target for Satan's attacks. There were constant attacks on Little Leroy in his valley of darkness and this acci-dent left him without hope. *"My days are swifter than a weaver's shuttle, and they come to an end without hope."* (Job 7:6 ESV)

He knew of my faith and he leaned on me. Whenever my brothers needed a miracle, they would call me and ask me to pray. *"Because He bends down to listen, I will pray as long as I have breath."* (Psalm 116:2 NLT) Every hell they went through I prayed, and God would answer by gifting them with a **precious moment.** God was always faithful and lifted them out of their hell.

After Vietnam, Little Leroy and Chief came to visit me in SLO. I felt the Holy Spirit prompting me to pray with them. I shared that God had told me He was going to reveal something special. They were both excited but wanted me to pray without them and give them the answer. I said, "God doesn't want it done like that." I suggested we drive to a hidden beach area. I love driving people in my car because I have a captive audience. It is the pulpit where I can build up faith and share how God has answered so many of my prayers. By the time we got to Avila, they were ready to pray with me. We sat, overlooking the beautiful ocean. They were both in their thirties, handsome, lean young men. As I held their hands and said The Lord's Prayer, I asked God to reveal what He wanted us to know. Immediately the Lord showed me a vision of the three of us flying a kite. One kite with all three of us holding one string, sharing it at the same time. I saw a large pair of scissors from heaven cut the string! It went from one kite to three kites…. The Lord showed me he had cut the kite string we were sharing and wanted each of us to fly our own kites, separately yet together. The Lord revealed that He wanted each of us to have a personal relationship with Him. God wanted them to grow in their prayer life and to depend on Him, not their sister. All three of us totally understood what the Lord was revealing. Previously my brothers came to me to pray, to pay, to give, or to organize their messes. From that time on, I can't remember my brothers coming to me for anything except for love.

For the next ten and more years the three of us were wrapped up in daily survival mode, being husbands, wives, parents, and life drama as many experience. Little Leroy was married five times, lived on an Indian reservation, and had one best friend from Vietnam. He had adopted out his daughters when he was a heroin addict believing that was a better future for them—and it was. Little Leroy was not only addicted to drugs, but he was also an alcoholic, which eventually led to his death. Before he went home to be with his Father, he still was not the father he hoped he could be. Because of his own abuse to himself, he didn't have what he wanted to give—love. He had children, friends, and wives he couldn't love, but he always gave them laughter till the day before he died.

His son, Fearless, was instrumental in prolonging Little Leroy's days, as Fearless had called me for the first time in his life and told me he didn't think his dad was going to live much longer and then hung up. That call was a confirmation of a dream I had. I knew when I woke up that day I needed to call my brother and ask how he was doing. He was on his deathbed; but when I called him, he acted jovial and told me he was fine. He was more concerned about me. Was I okay?

I told him that Jesus wanted me to call him. Little Leroy told me to tell Jesus hi for him. Again, Little Leroy in his humorous mode.

When I got off the phone with Little Leroy, the Lord told me to go see him...tomorrow. Of course the Lord knew I had a job, but I have found that when I obey God, He always makes a way for me to get to the other side of whatever He is wanting me to do. I always know when God talks to me, because He is loud in my spirit and I can't focus on anything else until I am obedient to His request. So I made plans to leave around three o'clock in the morning to get from Long Beach to San Joaquin. I had called my Aunt D and asked if I could stop by and visit as she lived in the area. She is my last long-living relative and now that I was older, we could banter back and forth. We loved those moments together even if they were far and few between.

So on this day, my aunt not only wanted to see me but she wanted me to pick her up before I went to Little Leroy's so she could surprise him also. I gladly picked her up and she knocked on his door first to pretend she came to visit and surprise him; but the biggest surprise was me from Long Beach. I stood right behind my Aunt D and we could hear Little Leroy say, "Who is it?" and Auntie said, "It's your Aunt D."

"Come in. Come in," he said, as he couldn't get off his couch. I peeked around my short Aunt D and Little Leroy started crying. As tears streamed down his cheeks, my aunt D said "Call 9-1-1."

My aunt was a retired nurse and she knew that Little Leroy was at the point of death. Little Leroy was on a couch, bloated like a blimp, tears streaming down his face. His legs looked like they had burst. If he wanted to go to the bathroom or get up and eat, it would have been impossible in his condition. The ambulance picked him up within minutes and we followed it to San Joaquin County Hospital, the same hospital where he had been born.

After many tests, Little Leroy was diagnosed with advanced cirrhosis of the liver and had about three months to live. If we had not shown up on that very day, we would have found him dead the very next day. Isn't that a **precious moment** to know that God does indeed talk to us? He directed my path and He saved my brother's life even if it was for only three months. It was three months that the Lord wanted to spend with Little Leroy drawing him back to Himself, our Good Shepherd who goes after the lost sheep. God also arranged for Little Leroy to be with people who loved him those last few months, like my son Strongwind and my grandsons Steven and Sebastian. All three of those hip men gave my brother warmth, love, and they laughed each time they were together.

San Joaquin County Hospital didn't want to pay for a 300-mile ambulance ride from San Joaquin to Long Beach and pretty much told me Little Leroy or I would be paying for that long-distance transport. Neither of us had the money; God made it happen! I was indignant that they wouldn't make sure he was near someone who could care for him! I told them Little Leroy was a Vietnam veteran who had earned a Purple Heart and I would go to the San Joaquin County Board of Supervisors, the VA Administrator and start calling local newspapers like the *San Joaquin Sun Star, Fresno Bee, San Francisco Chronicle* and tell my brother's story to all of them if he didn't get an ambulance ride. He needed his sister to take care of him and I lived in Long Beach. The next day after discussing the situation with hospital administration, they decided it was in the best interest of Mr. Yanez to send him to Long Beach VA hospital in an ambulance.

After the transfer, Little Leroy spent nearly a week in the Long Beach VA hospital where he sharpened his joke skills making my son Strongwind, daughter Songbird, and me laugh even though he knew he had only months to live. *"A cheerful heart is good medicine, but a crushed spirit dries up the bones."* (Proverbs 17:22 NIV)

ANSWERS TO PRAYERS

"But Jesus said to him, 'No one, after putting his hand to the plow and looking back, is fit for the kingdom of God.'"

LUKE 9:62 NASB

While Little Leroy and I were alone, he told me he had a few regrets in life, and if he could, he would have loved to visit more of the United States since he had fought for her. He regretted never meeting the daughters he had given up when he was a heroin addict. He longed to tell all his children he was sorry that he wasn't a good father; that he was exceedingly regretful for not being a man they could count on and admire.

He shared his dying wishes: "I wish I could see the United States and find my lost adopted daughters and spend time with my children." And my comment, as always, was "Let's pray!" "Father, in Jesus' name, please open doors which only you can open and if it is your will for my brother to find his girls and see the United States, please open those door, amen!"

My wheels were spinning in motion and I was talking to Jesus telling Him that I believed he didn't bring me this far to shut the doors in my brother's face, and this would be the perfect opportunity for us to spend time with Him. My brother made a pact with me before we left

San Joaquin County Hospital. If he agreed to be taken care of by me, I promised not to preach to him. I promised and therefore kept my mouth shut regarding Jesus.

The Lord opened a door from my job at the trucking company where I could get back on the road as a truck driver and I could take a passenger! Little Leroy filled out the necessary documents and signed up to be my passenger on the truck. We were off to see the United States and locate his missing adopted children!

We did indeed find one of his daughters in Riverside County on our way out of California. Praise Jesus! He got to hug and enjoy Aline and meet her boyfriend, Henry. Without a doubt that was a **precious moment**. Little Leroy also got to meet his son and daughter-in-law in Utah and the grandchildren he had never met before. Our God is so good! Although God didn't heal Little Leroy physically, He was healing him emotionally and spiritually and He healed broken relationships!

I was Little Leroy's nurse on an eighteen-wheeler and kept my mouth shut about Jesus until one day he confronted me and it changed his life forever! It happened on the third day of driving truck. I had to fuel up and this was also when I would dump Little Leroy's porta-potty. It was hard for him to get up and down out of the truck, so I had made the twin bed area convenient for him with a refrigerator full of his needs and desires, CDs to his delight, a soft pillow, heater, lights, coffee pot, microwave—he had it all; and of course he had to take his medicine which was prolonging his life. He hated the taste of it and acted like he hated me for making him take it. Anyway on the third day, I got out of my nice cold cab area vs. his raging hot twin bed area, stretched my legs, and bought us some fried chicken, his favorite at the time. After I fueled my truck, I was planning to wake him and surprise him with the fried chicken.

When I got back into the truck, he was sitting in the passenger seat, bundled up like a snowman. That sight tickled my funny bone and I started laughing. I knew he bundled up with a knit hat, snow gloves, army jacket with the hood on, and also his sleeping bag wrapped around him to emphasize how cold the cab of my truck was, which was nothing compared to the stone-cold silence of not speaking about Jesus.

So I waited for his comment after I stopped laughing, knowing he would say something which would bring me into another fit of laughter. He just had a special flair for making people laugh. He said, "Go ahead, Sis, lay it on me, I know you want to say something about God. What is it? I can't take it any longer!" I started laughing, but he was serious.

I said, "Brother, since we got into the truck together I only hear God repeating one sentence."

He said, "What the blank is it? Let's get this over with so I can enjoy my trip!"

"Here it goes, Brother: 'How does a man plow a field when he is always looking backwards?'"

His comment, "Sis, that doesn't make any sense at all. What the hell does that mean?"

I replied, "Do you remember the days you sat on Mr. H's' tractor?"

He said, "How could I forget? Of course I remember."

"Well, Brother, I think the Lord is asking you how would that field look if, as you sat on the tractor and plowed the field, your head was always turned backward? What would your field look like?"

He said, "It would be messed up!"

"In other words, Brother, all your life you seem to be looking at your past instead of your future! How does a man plow a field when he is always looking backward?"

If you have ears to hear this, then you have read a message from our Father.

At that moment, Little Leroy started crying and the color of his skin went from darkness into light and he wanted to live for the first time. He wanted to register for a liver-transplant. He also asked why I never told him that earlier in his life. I said, "Brother, most all of our family doesn't want me speaking about Jesus, but I am sure this is what Jesus wanted you to hear at this moment in your life."

While on the road after so many miles, a driver must stop for 32 consecutive hours. I planned to take that 32 hours and get Little Leroy to a casino, which meant renting a car from wherever I parked my big rig. Little Leroy had told me one of his dreams was to drive a brand-new white Cadillac, which he knew was impossible. He had a bum leg since he tried to commit suicide by driving off a cliff only to have the open driver door land on his leg. His driving days were pretty much over, but with God all things are possible!

I knew the truck stop I was headed to for my 32 hours time off and made arrangements with the truck-stop manager to park my rig and have a rented white Cadillac parked in the back of his truck stop; however, I let Little Leroy believe we could only find a messed-up Pinto to take us to a casino. He was fine with that, and when we drove up to the truck stop, Little Leroy pointed out the Pinto which was owned by one of the truck stop employees who was part of this gag I was playing on Little Leroy. The truck staff crew knew that my brother had only months to live and I had planned this adventure to grant his dying wish. They were all happy to participate.

Little Leroy loved to play poker. He had been getting ready for hours and when we stopped he couldn't wait to get in the Pinto. I told my brother I was going inside to shower, but really I went to meet the manager. We staged ourselves in the store to watch Little Leroy's reaction, we didn't expect Little Leroy to hurry out of my truck and try to get into the Pinto. He walked with a cane and was sick as a dog, so getting inside a car and sitting down was critical. We could see Little Leroy with a lit cigarette, trying to open the locked passenger door of the Pinto. He was cussing when he couldn't open it and struggled to get to the driver door. He lit up his second cigarette while he had one in his mouth, then he was looking around for me. He saw lots of people looking out the window at him and tried real hard to smile but I could see the fret on his face, so I quickly went outside and asked him, "What are you doing, Brother?"

He said, "What the heck does it look like, Sis?"

Then the manager drove the white Cadillac and parked it next to the Pinto and handed Little Leroy the keys. Little Leroy spit out his cigarette and asked, "Is this a joke?" I can still visualize Little Leroy's face as this whole event unfolded and it still makes me chuckle.

"Yes, Brother, the Pinto was the joke, but the Cadillac is a gift for you for a few days." First he sat down and cried and both of us cried knowing these were his last days and he was receiving more blessings and he knew only God could have made all this possible. He was so sorry he hadn't lived with Jesus earlier and understood why I had.

He only drove for about five miles and wanted to enjoy every moment of his ride and his surroundings. We went to a casino known for its 'all you can eat crab legs' and we ate until our stomachs hurt. Little Leroy gambled until he was ready to retire back to our bedroom on wheels, my truck; but I had booked a room for the night and allowed my brother to gamble while I took my bath and relaxed in our room for two!

It was such a miracle to have met his daughters, his son and daughter-in-law, and his grandkids, then travel the USA together. But the biggest surprise of all (and only God could have made this happen) was Little Leroy reconnecting with his one and only best friend from Vietnam.

We traveled twenty-eight states, as Winners Circle allowed me to make up my own route as long as the loads got to their destination on time. I tried to calculate as many states as I could while Little Leroy was alive. The days on the truck were profitable to hear his life story. We didn't realize how tragic our lives were until that truck adventure. We cried, laughed, prayed, and hoped for a miracle.

Little Leroy woke up one morning when we were in the Eastern part of United States and said, "Sis, do you think we can go home so I can sleep without moving?"

I said, "Of course."

So I started speaking to Jesus again about making provisions for Little Leroy to be home and for me to have favor at my job so I could take care of Little Leroy and his needs. It was too late in Little Leroy's diagnosis for him to be put on a liver-transplant list. He needed around-the-clock care as only a convalescent hospital could provide. Meanwhile

I had to get back on the road, but only for short trips so I could care for my brother's needs.

During the week or two at a convalescent hospital in Long Beach, my son Strongwind would pick up his uncle and take him to a movie and buy him his favorite milkshake. Little Leroy and Strongwind would shoot the breeze. During those conversations, my son learned that Little Leroy was being mistreated and not being taken care of properly. Of course Strongwind told me, and I looked for another place for Little Leroy. It wasn't until the third place that we found a convalescent hospital where Little Leroy felt comfortable. It was in Orange County and Little Leroy was happy.

The doctors had told Little Leroy he needed to quit smoking. He told me he had given up cigarettes but in truth the nurses confided that he and another patient smoked in a little hidden place outside their facility. He was dying so I didn't say anything and let him have his small pleasure. The nurses loved having my brother as their patient. He flirted with the nurses and made them laugh. The nurses told me that he and his other buddy would chase them in their wheelchairs. It brightened everyone's day.

I found out that this friend was from Ohio and had been an orderly in the Vietnam War. He was terminally ill like Little Leroy. Little Leroy and his friend didn't recognize each other, they had changed so much over thirty years. As they told their Vietnam stories to each other it finally dawned on them, they had actually been best friends in Vietnam! What an amazing discovery!

How is it that God knew they would both be sick at the same time; that He would bring Little Leroy's best friend all the way from Ohio so Little Leroy could love his best friend until his dying days? Only God could have arranged all these closing events for my brother. Certainly you have to agree that this was indeed a **"precious moment in hell"** for my brother, for his best friend, for his family, and for me.

My brother lived for nearly four months and had me seek out his children while he spent his last days in the Long Beach hospital.

Unfortunately his eldest son didn't get to say goodbye to his dad, but he helped me plan his dad's funeral.

Little Leroy had wanted to be buried in a military uniform. Leroy Jr. and I were both on a hunt to find a military uniform, yet it seemed absolutely no matter what we did, there was going to be no uniform. Little Leroy was thin when he passed, so size wasn't the problem but we just couldn't find one. Leroy Jr. went his way and I went mine. We both arrived at the same suit which was corduroy. Corduroy wasn't something Little Leroy ever wore, but we both seemed to love this particular corduroy suit and agreed he would be buried in it.

Then came the funeral parlor and we had to choose a coffin. There were books and pages of all types of coffins, hundreds to choose from. I found one which I thought was just what Little Leroy would have chosen, but I kept my thoughts to myself as I felt the ultimate decision should rest with his son. I left the room to give Leroy Jr. time to choose. When I returned, he had chosen the very one that was in my heart. The name of that coffin was Viceroy!

We hadn't set out to find clothing or a coffin which had my brother's name on it; it just happened. Leroy Jr. and I were in total agreement even though I hadn't spent any time with him since he was in a crib. What is the likelihood of all this falling into place without divine intervention?

It was the hand of God. He is our Precious Moments, and He gets all the Glory! Little Leroy may have been a broken down Vietnam veteran, but he died a Child of God!

NATIVE AMERICAN ROOTS

*"Yet who knows whether you have come to the kingdom for such
a time as this?"*

ESTHER 4:14 NKJV

My brothers' foray into the hells of alcoholism and drugs took them to the pits of despair. Watching their pain and suffering was enough to convince me not to travel that road. Don't get me wrong: I desire adventure, but not in those valleys of doom and gloom. Wide are the ways of the world but narrow is His path. If I have a choice in which direction to travel, I am forever going to choose adventures that God sends me on; adventures where I can grow, adventures which provide opportunities to help others.

As I was getting older and looking for a way to use the talents I had been given to make a better life for myself and my children, I got involved in my Native American community. Not because I knew much about my Native American heritage, but because I knew that it was an opportunity to help others. So I got involved in the plight of the people and decided to walk across America with my fellow Native Americans to Washington, DC.

As a participant of the march, we had to prepare. The leaders of the community wanted us to attend a pow-wow prior to going on the journey.

I was also the representative for San Joaquin Community College where I was attending. The reporter for the San Joaquin Sun Star local newspaper asked to go along with me for a story. He was handsome, single, and drove a Porsche. How could I say no? I was a single mother of two but I was still young and looked forward to having a little fun while attending the powwow. The Native American College leaders had agreed to allow the reporter to come with me to ensure that he would have factual information for the newspaper article. We decided to meet ahead of time so he could review what would be happening with the walk across America. In truth I didn't fully know what would happen or exactly what to expect, but in my mind I thought perhaps my life of turmoil was preparation for a time like this. Perhaps my survival as a loner would give me the strength to walk across America and speak to President Carter. I had often seen American Indians as people who were quiet people, and by God's authority and His presence in my life, I wanted to speak on their behalf. Just like God gave David the bravery to confront Goliath, I thought God would give me courage to stand with or for my people!

When we arrived, it was nearly dusk. There were hundreds of people, all types, not only Native Americans but others who supported their right, when we got out of car we thought we spotted Dennis Banks and Russel Mead, both of whom were being watched by the FBI for activities in South Dakota. I had no idea who they were as I had only recently become part of this community.

We were herded like cattle to a couple of different sweat lodges. I didn't know what those were either, but life is all about learning so I tugged the sleeve of the reporter and pulled him along with me toward the lodges. There were four to my recollection and one was set up exclusively for committed walkers. That was the tent I went in. As I entered the sweat lodge, the reporter waited outside for me; he was not allowed inside.

The event was called "The Longest Walk" and it was the first of its kind. The organizers had special regulations and instructions; the first one being that all walkers were to be cleansed in a sweat lodge before undertaking the walk. I'm not sure what I actually expected but I thought there would have been hundreds committed to the walk; that night there were less than a dozen people who entered that lodge, and I was the only woman. Surely God had allowed certain experiences in my life for such a time as this, right?

The lodge was short, circular, built over dirt, and the center had a pit dug out with hot rocks burning in the middle. I let all the men enter first so I could get a seat close to the exit; my seat turned out to be across from their shaman. I had to constantly rub my eyes because I was sweating and my mascara was running. Eventually, I rubbed my eyes so much on the towel provided, I wasn't wearing any more mascara. The shaman was the spokesperson for our group and told us that the "great spirit" would enter and speak to all of us. He also said we would sing in unison when it entered... My skepticism kicked in as I thought, "Yeah, right! How could we sing in unison if we were all strangers and only three of the people in the lodge had ever experienced a sweat lodge? Impossible!" But the shaman spoke in a loud and thunderous voice, saying, "It has entered." It nearly scared me to death when he yelled that. I rubbed my eyes again so I could get a better view of what was hovering over the rocks. I could see something like a clear balloon, approximately 12" in diameter. I put my hand out to touch it, but was instructed to just listen. I was told when the spirit spoke, it would talk to each of us individually and that we needed to share what it was saying to each of us. It started speaking to the men to the side of the shaman. As each man was spoken to, they told the words that were spoken to them and it all pointed to me. One spoke and said, "The woman has been chosen to be the mother of the march and wherever she goes, there will be protection." Another spoke and said, "wherever the woman is the owl will follow us and will have covering from the elements." Oh, yes we did sing a few minutes in unison. I could pick up the tune but the words were foreign to me. When the spirit was done speaking, the shaman had everyone exit the hut except me. He wanted to know who I was, where I was from, and my name. He asked me question after question. I just wanted out of that hut and to go back to the reporter's car.

When the shaman was finally done questioning me, I left the hut and found the reporter standing outside waiting for me next to the sweat lodge. He wanted to know what had happened because the men who were exiting the lodge were talking about the woman inside and I was the only woman. I told him I didn't really know exactly what just happened; all I knew was that the shaman said that I was chosen by this spirit to be the "mother of the march."

Before I left, the shaman told me that a few men from his tribe would be at my door tonight to give further instructions. I informed him that I was not giving anyone my home address. I didn't know these men—they were complete strangers. I had children at home so I was very protective and my background had taught me to be distrusting. This was all foreign to me and I admit I was a little shaken and somewhat afraid. I told this shaman that I didn't feel comfortable letting anyone know where I lived until I found out more about what just happened. In other words, I needed to get home and talk to Jesus. The reporter had his story and I had a new life mission with people I knew nothing about. I just wanted to join the cause of the Native Americans to help my people. I needed Jesus to tell me that this was okay.

I got home around 11:30 PM. I heard a hard knock at my front door. I thought perhaps it was the reporter who had forgotten to tell me something or wanted to chat. But there they stood, two large Native American men standing at my door. I did not want to talk to them. I slammed the door in their faces. How in the world did they know where I lived? Before I had left, the shaman had said that Native Americans didn't need addresses, they always found their way. And sure enough, there they were! I had been so confused and a bit frightened when we left the powwow. I made certain no one was tailing us. The entire drive home we continuously looked over our shoulders and in the rear view mirror to ensure we were not followed.

I cannot remember the name of the reporter but his story was written in the February 2, 1978 issue of the San Joaquin Sun Star. After the Sun Star printed their story, I became a bit of a local star. Not that I asked for or wanted such a thing, but in the back of my mind I recalled stories in the Bible about Moses, Joseph, David, and others who didn't run for office. Their leadership positions were appointed because they loved and trusted God. They had faith the size of a mustard seed and God chose them for His purpose. I thought God was planning to use me to help these people. The Native Americans had one agenda; God had another.

For the next few months I was involved in more powwows, raising money, participating in ceremonies on Alcatraz Island, etc. Musicians donated their talents for the cause. I just wanted to march and talk to President Carter.

The night that our walk began from Sacramento to Nevada, a few of the Native Indian women stopped the march and insisted I be ousted or they would not walk. The march wasn't moving until the security guards walked me to the end of the trail of cars. I was heartbroken! I believed that God had chosen me for this mission. Some of the Native Americans had believed their great spirit chose me. All I knew was that I wanted to march, I wanted to make a difference. However, the women said that I didn't know their ways and that my God was not theirs.

The two guards now turned into three and they walked me to the end of the march. I sat down in the middle of nowhere, near the Nevada summit. If God had sent me on this mission, no security guards were going to stop me from trailing behind them. Besides, they had my car filled with their supplies. Midnight and it was pitch-black outside. I didn't know where I was, but I had made up my mind that after the marchers pulled out, I would trail behind them. As I sat on the curb, I experienced a strange feeling come over me, almost like a clear balloon over me as I cried my heart out. Here I was, rejected again, through no fault of my own. All I had on me were my clothes; no flashlight, no car keys, no car, nothing ... just me and Jesus again.

I believe with all my heart that Jesus never leaves me or forsakes me. If He allowed this to happen I knew there was a purpose. After I finished praying, I felt that balloon lift. As I stood up a car stopped. The driver asked if I needed help. He said he stopped because it looked like I was injured. Little did I know that this man was on his way to commit suicide. I accepted the ride and while I sat in the passenger seat describing what had just happened, I asked him if he had seen an Indian march roll through. I couldn't hear his reply. I was totally focused on the vision God was suddenly giving me. I told him that I had this vision of a man who was in the car with us. I explained to this driver that God had given me a few gifts, one of them being visions. The driver asked me to give a description of the man. I told him he was tall like Abraham Lincoln, thin, and was wearing a brown brimmed hat pulled down over his forehead. He was leaning on a tree with one foot on the tree, almost standing on one foot. Kind of how you see cowboys leaning on fences. The man started crying and had to pull over. He sobbed as he told me that I had just described his father to him. He said he was on his way to meet his dad. Then I told him that in my vision, his dad was teary eyed and I asked him why he would be sad. The driver told me he was planning to drive off a cliff to be with his dad. His dad had died a few years ago. They had been best friends. I didn't know why Jesus chose me for that moment in this man's life, but before I got out of the car, I asked him if I could pray with him. I prayed the Our Father prayer and then asked God for His will to be done. God intervened! That man didn't kill himself; instead he went home to his wife and two sons. To God's glory, He gifted me with visions and on this night Jesus allowed me to see the vision of this man's dad in order to save this man's life.

Perhaps my whole involvement with the Native American march was so I could meet this man on this journey? I often use the words "for such a time as this" because God has woven our stories and lives so that we are at the right place and time in order to accomplish His will if we submit ourselves to Him. I believe my story was woven into this man's life for just such a time as this!

I requested to be dropped off near the railroad tracks. I figured that the train runs to Nevada and by morning, perhaps I would find the march.

I found a train tunnel and slept in it for the night. Luckily I found that spot. As soon as I walked into the tunnel it started pouring down rain. Remember what the "spirit" in the powwow with the shaman said: wherever I was I would be sheltered from the elements. When I woke up the next morning and stepped out of the tunnel, on the other side I was overlooking the march folks. They were sleeping in garbage bags and trying to shelter themselves from the rain, yet I was dry. Some of the people below saw me and seemed happy as they pointed to me. Not all of the people in the march were involved in the decision to leave me behind, just a few women. They could see I was dry and under protection while they, being led by the other women, were not sheltered. Even so, three of those security guards made their way up the hill with a vehicle and gave me an ultimatum: I could turn around and go home because they did not know me and I had no name, or I could accidentally fall from the cliff which I stood upon. Immediately I had a vision. I saw a woman dressed in white Native American attire, similar to a wedding dress. She showed me that she was hidden under leaves, as if she had been tossed. She seemed to be warning me that these men would do what they said they were going to do. Because of that vision, I turned around and pretended to leave the march. They left me alone, but when the march was out of sight, I continued to Nevada and rented a room. I called the San Joaquin Sun Star and told them I had been ousted from the march because of my belief in Jesus.

When I read the article the Sun Star wrote about me being ousted from the march, I remembered the angel who said, "You know who your father is because they will treat you the same way they treated Him." What better way to end a story except for the cause of Jesus. The Native Americans have many ways that I know are not from the Bible; they conjure up a spirit with chants, herbs, and dead animals, and it was true my God was not theirs. Yet God still used me for His purpose even when I stepped into a valley that I had no business being in.

I was given talents and was able to use them to bring and deliver hope to the broken and lost and the story written in Sun Star was an impetus for other Christians to want to meet me. So I was able to find like-minded people to fellowship with. My God's purpose will not be thwarted. *"For the LORD Almighty has purposed, and who can thwart him? His hand is stretched out, and who can turn it back?"* (Isaiah 14:27 NIV)

AUNT D AND THE RING

"Put on the full armor of God, so that you can take your stand against the devil's schemes."

EPHESIANS 6:11 NIV

I have learned we are missing true blessings if we are not spending time in God's word. He has so much to say to us and His word never comes back void.

In Matthew 17:20 ESV we are told, *"He said to them, "Because of your little faith. For truly, I say to you, if you have faith like a grain of mustard seed, you will say to this mountain, 'move from here to there,' and it will move, and nothing will be impossible for you."*

My Aunt D was experiencing the most challenging month of her life the same summer as I was ending my mission with the Native Americans. She called me out of the blue, which was extremely unusual. No one in my family ever called me except Little Leroy or Chief, my brothers. For my aunt to have my phone number is odd as well, but for some reason God only knows, she called and I answered. She indicated she would like to come over for coffee or tea or just to chat but I sensed there was more. As soon as I got off the phone, I started praying. My Aunt D believed I had a special anointing on my life because I had survived so much. She was also convinced I had to be a faithful Christian, to her that I was a

Christian after all the newspapers said that I was ousted from the march because of my belief in Jesus. I always say that what Satan means for bad, God can use for His glory. Even though my heart broke when I was rejected at the march, I knew God allowed it. Just as God had allowed Job to endure enormous turmoil, yet Job was never forsaken by God and neither was I.

So here I was in my tiny two-bedroom home on the right side of the tracks of San Joaquin. As a matter of fact, you could step outside my back door and walk right onto the railroad tracks. I say that I was on the right side of the tracks because I grew up on the "wrong side of the tracks," but this is not only a reference to the physical location but also my spiritual one. I was now raising my children alone, living on the physically right side of the tracks as well as walking with God on the right side. God is merciful and helps the downtrodden. Through His grace and mercy, I was able to bring my family out of the dark valley and into the light. I have been adopted by our Almighty Father and I am a daughter of the King of kings who bestowed me with spiritual gifts. He had plans to use those gifts in my Aunt D's life.

Many thoughts rushed through my head about what my Aunt D wanted. I remembered all she had done for my brothers and me when we were teenagers. She had taken the three of us in when she already had three children of her own, giving her a half dozen to feed and care for. She was now raising her grandchildren because their mother was in prison. My aunt had the heart of a nurse, always trying to fix people and families. She had a big heart but she was short on patience. Providing an atmosphere of peace was definitely not her strong suit. My Aunt D was a champ of sarcasm, but as teenagers we needed empathy not sarcasm. She always had an agenda. My aunt did everything with a purpose. She didn't like wasted time; hers or yours. If something needed to be done, then she expected us to do it and didn't tolerate us watching TV or relaxing. She would tell us that it was "rude and selfish … and to get our lazy bum up and make something, do something, or get out of her sight." That was who she was. So as teenagers, although she took care of us, we all learned to avoid her. This is all to explain that my aunt D and I had a complicated relationship and we didn't always see eye to eye.

When she arrived at my door, I anticipated her normally tough demeanor and sarcastic comments. I was unprepared for the way she entered. She walked in humbly, her shoulders slumped down, her head bowed, and gobs of Kleenex in both hands. She was broken and teary eyed. Her posture took me by surprise because my aunt was the strongest person I knew on my mother's side of the family. My aunt was imperfect, as we all are, but she was a "born-again, spirit-filled Christian." Even though we didn't agree on much, we did agree on "who our father was."

I placed my arms around her shoulders and tried to soothe her but as I did that she shrugged off my arms and said, "Where's that coffee you said you were going to make?" She sat herself at my counter. I poured her a cup of coffee and had everything at the table so she could fix it up the way she liked it. That morning my aunt drank it black. She nibbled on my little tray of cookies. I noticed that she had rings on every finger and even two on some fingers. Aunt D didn't wear cheap jewelry. She didn't do cheap anything. She may not have always been able to purchase what she wanted but she did what she could to get the best whenever possible.

She kept asking me about the Native American march and the events leading up to me being ousted. It was all just small talk as I knew she had something on her mind. This morning she was clearly beside herself and I suggested that before she started talking, perhaps we could pray first so we could call on the Holy Spirit for such a time as this. She said, "Yes, Mija." I asked Jesus to give us His wisdom and fill us with His presence, in Jesus name, amen! That's my prayer of faith the size of a mustard seed. Then she spoke.

She told me her son hung himself, her house was robbed, and her car was stolen all in the same month. She said she couldn't take it any longer and that she just wanted to die and didn't understand why God, whom she trusted, allowed all this madness into her world when she tried so hard to be a good person. She had experienced a divorce. She was help-ing her kids who were no longer kids but adults now. She was raising her grandchildren. A lot of burden and stress poured out as she talked and cried. I suddenly realized I couldn't hear her, I saw her lips moving but I was focused on one ring on her finger. It just stood out. Not because it was large or vibrant but the Lord had my focus on that one ring. I had to stop her from her story and I asked her where she got that particular ring. She asked if I liked it and said I could have it. It was topaz with diamonds. I said, "No thank you, Auntie, but Jesus wants me to ask you about that one ring." She said that ring was given to her by her ex-husband Richard's girlfriend. "Isn't that nice of her?"

My response was, "how long have you had that ring, Auntie"?

She said, "Around a month now."

Aunt D had a ring which was cursed and was meant to do intentional harm to her and her household. I know it sounds creepy and most people shy away from what they don't understand. I can only tell you what my ears were hearing and what my Lord told me to do. The Bible says that we have an adversary, the devil, who is intent on inflicting harm and destruction upon unsuspecting Christians. This is why we are warned to be on guard against the devil's schemes. God's power is greater than Satan. In Micah 5:12 NIV the Lord says, *"I will destroy your witchcraft and you will no longer cast spells,"* so we don't need to be afraid. We only need to lean into Him for protection but we must know who our enemy is and put on the full armor of God. *"Put on the full armor of God, so that you can take your stand against the devil's schemes."* (Ephesians 6:11 NIV)

"Auntie, we need to get rid of that ring and send it back to the pits of darkness."

My demoralized aunt D changed into a warrior. She and I got up from the kitchen and proceeded to my back yard to throw that ring onto the railroad tracks. The ground at the tracks was always so hard that you could water for months and it wouldn't soften. It was like a giant rock under the tracks. My auntie's ring was stuck on her finger. She was swabbing it with her spit, trying to twist it off with her teeth, pushing, pulling and it would not budge. Meanwhile, I was praying and asking Jesus to send this ring back to the pits of darkness in Jesus' name and I pled the Blood of Jesus on my aunt D and her household, and for Satan to get thee behind me. I asked again, "Father, in Jesus' name we ask you to send this ring back to the pits of darkness." As I said that, my aunt's ring flew off her finger and plunged to the ground. The ground literally opened up and swallowed the ring! My aunt and I looked at each other in shock. We were flabbergasted! We both witnessed that ground open up to the size of a two-inch hole, swallow up that ring, and close back up again like it had never opened. Our intention was to throw it over the railroad tracks but our ways are not God's ways and His way was much, much better.

Many years later, I read these words, *"And the earth opened her mouth and swallowed them up..."* (Numbers 26:10 KJV) which jumped off the page of my Bible; that is exactly what happened to that ring! God's almighty power is beyond our comprehension.

After God's miraculous intervention in destroying that ring, my aunt D's problems ceased. She became an officer in the Salvation Army until she quit to parent her grandchildren.

This is one of those situations that Satan meant for evil but God turned around for His glory. It was a **precious moment in hell!**

VISIONS AND DREAMS—222

And in the last days it shall be, God declares, that I will pour out my Spirit on all flesh, and your sons and your daughters shall prophesy, and your young men shall see visions, and your old men shall dream dreams."

ACTS 2:17 ESV

Where do I start? I have been gifted with visions and dreams. *"We have different gifts, according to the grace given to each of us...."* (Romans 12:6 NIV) I was only eight years old when God began giving me visions and dreams in preparation for events which were about to unfold. I realize there may be some who won't understand or believe how God has worked in me, but I cannot deny what I have experienced. I also recognize that after reading certain accounts in my life, some may think they are fabricated stories. But like the apostle Paul, I assure you before God that I am telling the absolute truth. *"Now in what I am writing to you, I assure you before God that I am not lying"* (Galatians 1:20 NASB)

Doesn't the Bible say that whosoever believes and has the faith of a mustard seed, he or she can move mighty mountains in Jesus' name? How do you move mighty spiritual mountains unless you can see them in the spiritual realm? That is where I believe my dreams and visions come from: His Heavenly realm.

This particular story has to do with a house in Laguna Hills, California, approximately six miles from Laguna Beach. I began having dreams and for nearly three years my dreams included the number 222. Every time I had that dream with 222, I would tell my children. They knew I had some special gifts involving dreams and visions so they were curious about what I thought the numbers meant? I could only guess, 2 people, 2 months, 222 dollars, 222 days or months or years? I had no clue, except those three 2's meant something. I knew God was trying to tell me something. He wanted me to be aware and equipped. I felt I needed to be prepared so I didn't miss out like in the parable of the virgins at the wedding feast (Matt. 25: 1–13). I believed our Helper, the Holy Spirit, was prepping me for something. He kept bringing this number to my mind—I just didn't yet know what He was prepping me for.

It wasn't unusual for the Lord to wake me up and tell me to get in my car and start driving. He often led me to a house I had never been to or an area I was not familiar with, and I would invariably meet someone in need. It has happened enough times that I know when He wakes me I just need to go.

It requires an act of faith and obedience to His beckoning. I know when He calls me, because He doesn't stop nudging me until I obey. It's not an option for me to say, "No, Lord, I am not going to say that." Or "No, Lord, I am not going there." I tried that once and it didn't work well for me. I said, "No way, Lord! Take this cup from me. I hate truck driving and I am NOT going to become a truck driver! No way!" Then the Lord shut every occupation for me for nearly 18 months until I surrendered and became a truck driver. It was either that or starve to death. Truck driving did become one of the most challenging and rewarding occupations I ever had. It turned out to be a pure blessing in many, many ways. It was also the means for allowing my veteran brother his dying wish to see the USA. But back to my dream of 222.

In this dream I could see a commercial zone, yet a few of the blocks were also homes. It was a short walk to a downtown area and was near the ocean. I remember in the dream a few people would ask, 'How did you find this place?" At the time I didn't know what place they were speaking about. Then I would wake up. The number 222 was in there somewhere.

At the time I lived in Seal Beach, California with my daughter Ebb and husband Willard. Willard and I were not doing well as a married couple. He was having affairs with other married women, which had taken me by surprise. It actually came as a bit of a shock the day the Lord allowed me to be bitten by a dog. I went home early from work and found him in bed with another woman! I began to pray that the Lord would guide me to find a safe and peaceful place for my daughter and me. Ebboni was starting high school and I wanted to get her settled into a home and new school as soon as possible.

One morning I awoke after having a clear dream that I just knew was from the Holy Spirit. In the dream I witnessed the clouds form into humongous praying hands and then into one almighty finger that was used like a pencil and wrote a scripture—Mark 2:11. I immediately grabbed my Bible to look up that verse. I wanted to see what God was trying to tell me: *"I say to you, 'Get up. Take your bed and go to your home.'"* (Mark 2:11 NLV). As soon as I read that scripture, I asked the Lord, "What do you want me to do?"

He said, "Get in your car and drive." I knew He meant now! I thought I was going to find someone in an automobile accident or perhaps a house on fire or some other emergency was going to happen. It felt urgent so I didn't even take time to change out of my pajamas, brush my teeth, comb my hair, or put on shoes. I just put on my slippers and got into my car. As soon as I sat in my car, I thought what am I doing and where am I going? Then the Lord said, "405 South." I got on the I-405 South believing the timing and destination was critical.

Since it was early morning, the traffic was beginning to pick up and I was expecting a broken-down car, an accident, someone on the side of the road—anything and everything was up for grabs. I never know where God is going to lead me or who He is leading me to. I just go.

I drove for a good twenty or so miles and nothing. Finally I got through Irvine, Lake Forest, cities I am not familiar with...and then I heard the Lord say, "Take a right." I pulled off on a street called Carlota. Carlota happens to be my name in Spanish. All the time I was still looking for a critical situation, still none. Then I ended up at a road called Ridge Route and turned onto it. I was following a large white pickup truck. It turned into a parking area and I felt I needed to follow it until it stopped and whoever got out of the truck must be the person who was needing prayer.

I tried to look inconspicuous but they could see I was the only other vehicle in their area and I happened to be parked behind them. When the woman got out of the truck, she was loaded with gear. She must have been close to six feet tall and heavy. She was heading into her office but walked up to my car and asked if she could help me. So to make small talk, the only thing that popped into my head was, "Do you have anything for rent?

She asked me, "Did you see a 'For Rent' sign?"

I said "No. How about anything for lease?"

She said, "Did you see a 'For Lease' sign?"

I answered, "No."

Then I said, "I have been led here and I don't expect you to believe me, but I know God has sent me here."

She responded, "Don't be too sure about me not believing you. You want to come in and have a cup of coffee?"

I replied, "I would love to. But I am still in my pajamas and haven't even brushed my teeth."

She said, "That's okay. We won't be getting that close and while the coffee is brewing you can tell me your story as I do believe in God leading people. I retired from being a nun before I accepted this job."

I told her about the dream of the clouds, folding hands, and His big finger in the sky writing the scripture Mark 2:11 that said for me to "*take your bed and go to your home.*"

She was very interested in my story and leaned back in her office chair, pulled out a set of keys from her desk drawer, and said, "I think these keys are for you. Now let me tell you a story."

"Last night, I got a phone call from the man who owns this house. He recently lost his wife and family and doesn't want his house anymore. He wants me to get rid of it for him. Go and look at this house and see if it's something you might be interested in."

I said, "I can't afford it even if I wanted it."

She said, "Oh, you of little faith. Do you think I am going to have a heart attack or stroke; or is my office going to go up in flames? Or do you believe God sent you here?"

I said, "I know God sent me here."

So I drove to the empty house and walked inside. It was everything I wanted and needed for Ebb-oni and me, especially the living room where I always wanted to have a big Bible study room for folks. I dropped to my knees in that living room and told Jesus, "Lord, if you want me to have this home, tell me what price to offer, and you know Lord I am between jobs and only have $1,200 to my name." As I asked the Lord that question, I could see in vision form "$10,000" written across the living room.

I drove back to the lady's office and told her what the Lord showed me. She spit out her coffee as if to choke on that answer and said, "Honey, nothing has sold here for less than $60,000 for as long as I can recall. That's not going to happen. But you know what, he wants to give his house away, so maybe he will accept that offer. I don't know."

"Can you call him? If it's God's will, it will be done."

She said, "Honey, he is on a bus this morning and I don't know that he will even answer his phone. He is so broken but I will dial." She dialed and he answered. She spoke briefly and told him I wanted to talk to him.

As she handed me the phone, I said, "Sir, your home is an answer to my prayer but all I have to offer is $1,000 today (it was October), By next tax time I should have more money. Would you accept $10,000 for your home?"

He said, "Sure."

Wow, I just bought a home in my pajamas! If I had been 30 minutes later, she might have put the house on the market or who knows what? I do know the timing was crucial and it was God's timing!

I gave her back the phone, she spoke with him a little more, and then hung up. She said, "God does work in mysterious ways."

I asked her if I could come back tomorrow and bring the cash and may I pray with her.

We prayed. I cried as I drove back to Seal Beach. I cried because God always takes such good care of me and this is just one of those additional miracles He made happen in my life.

As soon as I got home, I called my son and told him I just bought a house, without money, in my pajamas! He was sure I was misinterpreting this massive transaction as he and his wife had just bought a home and it was an ordeal. He took off work the following day and went to Laguna Hills with me. His wife Veronica went, too.

We drove to the manager's office. Sure enough, I handed her a check for $1,000 and she handed me the keys. I was so excited, scared, beside myself. Telling this story over and over again thrills me.

My son, Strongwind, is a man whom I trust. He has the ability to discern, so I take his word to heart. He examined the home outside first as Veronica and I examined the inside. All of a sudden I heard my son yell, "Mom! Mom come outside quick!" He said, "Mom look at the number on your mail box: 222!" Praise Jesus! Thank you, Jesus, is all we could say.

I am still in awe of this amazing story God wove into my life! Guided by a dream to a home near a commercial zone, within walking distance to the mall, and not far from Laguna Beach, with an address of 222—just like my dreams. Not to mention a vision for the price, the street called Carlota, a realtor who had been a nun and believed in God's divine leading, and a man who was willing to sell me a $60,000 home for only $10,000!

But I still needed $10,000 and I didn't have it, nor did I have friends or family to borrow it from; plus I was between jobs. Well, three days after I quietly bought this home, the local sheriff deputies knocked on my door seeking Charli. I didn't know what to expect, but I said I was Charli. They asked me to sign a document that showed they had made a special delivery.

When I sat down, first with a cup of coffee so I could be geared up, I slowly opened it expecting the worst. But it was good news: the Lord had collected back child support of nearly $12,000. I was holding my house payment plus a little extra cash!

When Ebb-oni and I moved in, she reminded me, "Mom, remember when we talked about moving somewhere and we prayed and asked God to give us a home where I could live for all my high school years? He gave us a home not a rental!" The Bible verse that jumps out at me is: *"Now to him who is able to do immeasurably more than all we ask or imagine...."* (Ephesians 3:20 NIV)

I have to say this whole event happened while Ebb-oni and I were experiencing hell with my late husband and the **precious moment** was God interceding.

DAUGHTER ABDUCTED, MOTHER MURDERED

"And do not fear those who kill the body but cannot kill the soul. But rather fear Him who is able to destroy both soul and body in hell."

MATTHEW 10:28 NKJV

There is a line from a 1958 movie, *The Inn of the Sixth Happiness*, starring Ingrid Bergman, which addresses a question many have found themselves asking at one time or another. In this conversation between a prison guard and Ingrid Bergman, the guard made the statement, "I have heard you have a God who protects you from harm." To which Ingrid Bergman responded, "It is the safety of the soul that my faith promises, not of the body." Our God has in fact promised the safety of our soul through Jesus' finished work on the cross and that eternal safety is available to all who believe, who repent of their sin, and accept Jesus Christ as their Lord and Savior.

We are not promised a pain-free life here on earth. I do not have a full answer for why God allows bad things to happen. All I can say is we live in a fallen world. God gave us choice and starting way back in the Garden of Eden when He gave Adam and Eve everything they could possibly need, He allowed them free choice to obey Him or not. God said, *"Of every tree of the garden you may freely eat; but of the tree of the knowledge of good and evil you shall not eat, for in the day that you eat of it you shall surely die."* (Genesis 2:16–17 NKJV) Along came Satan to temp man, much like today, he twisted the truth. First Satan asked, *"Did God really say, 'You must not eat from any tree in the garden'?"* (Genesis 3:1 NIV) Then He lied, *"You will not certainly die."* (Genesis 3:4 NIV) Adam and Eve both made the choice to believe Satan rather than God because, *"When the woman saw that the fruit of the tree was good for food and pleasing to the eye, and also desirable for gaining wisdom, she took some and ate it. She also gave some to her husband, who was with her, and he ate it."* (Genesis 3:6 NIV) In other words, they chose to disobey God in order to satisfy their own pleasures. Sin entered our world—this is known as "the fall." We each have choices in life and because we live in a fallen world, even the wrong choices of others can and do impact us, so sometimes bad things even happen to what we consider "good" people. Actually, I don't know a single person other than Jesus Christ, who has walked on this earth and never ever committed a sin. The Bible says, *"For all have sinned and fall short of the glory of God"* (Romans 3:23 NIV). It also says, *"For the wages of sin is death, but the gift of God is eternal life in Christ Jesus our Lord"* (Romans 6:23 NIV). So our concept of "good" people is clearly different from God's. Yet He loves us! How do I know this? Because He told me and He has shown me. *"But God demonstrates his own love for us in this: While we were still sinners, Christ died for us."* (Romans 5:8 NIV)

I have procrastinated writing this story realizing this morning it brings me to shame, pain, and regret. My pain is increased thinking my daughter's abduction might have been prevented if perhaps I had made different decisions. My poor choices began years before the actual abduction. First with my own mother Lupe who loved to party with anyone, anywhere and anytime, which makes me consider what the devil's den must look like; yet I put my little Songbird in the clutches of that very demon not knowing there is such a thing as a wolf in sheep's clothing.

Songbird was only nine months old when she and I were on our own without her father to care for us. He abruptly left us for another woman, no warning, no clue. The home where we were living was free as long as my husband was working on the farm. Since he no longer came to work, we no longer had a home. I certainly couldn't call Mrs. H and ask for her help. How would it look that I married a man at my young age of nineteen and now had a baby and no place to live? It was easier to call Lupe and see if she would allow us to stay at her home for a few weeks while I looked for my first job and begged an employer to take me on. To her credit, Lupe didn't hesitate. Her house was clean, my half brothers and sisters had clean clothes on, and they each had their own bed. That was an improvement but Lupe was still the party animal.

Songbird was my easiest birth, blonde hair, blue-hazel eyes, and the round happy, gentle face of a dove. When I was a little girl I asked God, "If I ever have children, please give me a blonde hair, blue-eyed, talented little girl and a tall, dark, handsome, athletic son." The Lord did, indeed. But I get ahead of myself. At this point in life, I now had a precious gift, a baby girl. I needed assistance in caring for her and I asked the party demon if she would take care of her while I went to my first day at work as a waitress at Denny's in San Joaquin. She was reluctant but gave me the green light.

Denny's hadn't had a help wanted sign. I was carrying my little gift of joy as I walked the streets of San Joaquin praying and asking God for help as I cried, filled with pain. Songbird's daddy left with another woman— why didn't he want Songbird and me? I was a good wife, good cook, good mommie, I painted two stories of interior paint making our home beautiful. I learned how to sew at Mrs. H's so I made curtains for every window, I got up every morning at 2:00 AM to make a hot breakfast for my husband, and I had a nice body. Why did your daddy leave us, Songbird?

I had no car, no money, no family: just me and my precious gift, Songbird. Actually Denny's was my last application and destination for the day and I sat at the counter and asked if I had to pay for water. The older woman behind the counter asked if I was hungry and fell in love with Songbird. She then asked, "What's going on? You look like you need a friend?" Well, I started to cry again as I nestled Songbird close to my heart. I didn't want her to cry too.

This sweet waitress who seemed like an angel to me told me I didn't have to fill out the application because they were not officially hiring; however, she thought she could put me on a graveyard position that was opening—would I consider taking it? If I said yes, she said she would train me and perhaps give me a bed for a week. It was a relief to be at an open door. The catch: I needed to be at work that evening around 4:00 PM before evening rush hour to start training. Yes was my answer! I cleared my voice and wiped my tears and ate the cheeseburger and fries. She blessed me—Songbird and I had a future. I was thankful that Denny's picked me up because it was walking distance from my mother's home.

It was early afternoon when I dragged myself back to Lupe's home. She was always harsh with me and continuously heaped guilt onto my shoulders. I tried to ignore whatever she threw at me but it's hard to avoid darkness when you walk into it! I hoped I could cheer her by loving on my new brothers and sister. It appeased her, but I could still feel her resentment. I don't remember her ever cuddling Songbird like most grandmothers do: she always seemed to be on a spin from one personality to another. Quick as a whip her mood would change from calm to nasty, so we had to tiptoe around on eggshells. "We don't want the devil to wake up, shhhhhh!" Even though my half brothers and sister ranged from three to six years old, they had already learned to stay away from her and keep still. Songbird never made a peep unless she was laughing. I don't remember her ever crying; she was such a perfect child.

So there I was, God had answered my prayers: I had a job and a new beginning. That was wonderful, yet I had mixed feelings about other things happening in my life and no good feelings about living at my mother's house, dependent on her help. But I had no place else to go so I made the move from the Watsonville farm to my hometown, San Joaquin—familiar grounds.

This may have been the beginning of Songbird's life of destruction. I still have some guilt and shame associated with the knowledge I had placed Songbird in the clutches of Satan and just hoped it would turn out okay.

I asked my mother if she would please watch her grandbaby for my first day. She agreed. I wasn't at work long when Denny's received a phone call looking for the mother of a little white baby girl who had been abandoned at their gas station with a note attached to her. The note stated that her mother, Charli, worked at Denny's. I couldn't believe it! Fortunately the gas station was only a few blocks from Denny's. I ran to the gas station and there was my bundle of joy, Songbird, sitting on the counter in her carrier, with her bottles and our bag of belongings. The gas station attendant didn't know what was going on. At that moment I hated my mother. How could she ... but today I have to ask myself, how could I?

Seven years later, I was a college student working part-time for the San Joaquin County Administrator as an intern administrator. My children wanted to visit their grandma Lupe. She had children they could play with, so when my brothers and sister asked if Songbird and Strongwind could spend a night I saw no harm in that. I innocently dropped them off and drove the 36 miles home. It seemed I had just gotten back home when the phone rang; Songbird wanted to come home. She said she wasn't feeling well and asked if would come get her. For Songbird to complain about anything was unusual, so I made the drive back around 10:00 PM.

When I picked them up, Strongwind fell asleep in the car, but Songbird was coy, quiet, distant, yet wanting to be under my arm while I drove. We didn't have the seat belt laws in those days. She wasn't crying, no temperature, yet she wasn't herself. I noticed when I picked them up that my mother wasn't home, just her kids—she had gone out to party. I don't know why I trusted she was different after all these years but my trust was misplaced. She hadn't changed her old habits—she had just perfected the art of masking her life.

When we got home, I put the two kids to bed. I wanted to talk to Songbird, but I considered she was probably tired after a long day playing. I know I was exhausted so I went to bed. As I started to doze off, I heard whimpering at my doorway; and there stood little Songbird. She told me she hurt down there. "Down where, honey?" She pointed at her panties. I didn't see anything and asked her, "What happened? Did you fall down today?" She said no, that her uncles touched her down there. "What! Oh no, no way!" I was beside myself in anguish. "Lord, did you really allow this to happen to your daughter Songbird, no way, Lord, no way, Lord!"

I lived next to the railroad tracks. I stepped out my door into my backyard and onto the tracks. I had a meltdown and began begging God to take my life. My children hurting was unbearable pain and I couldn't take it anymore. It was too much. I didn't want to live. "Please take me home, Jesus, please!" He didn't allow a train. Both my little ones were standing out in the dark crying, watching their momma cry and afraid their momma was going to get run over by the choo choo train. I saw them and I started singing, "Jesus loves me this I know." Somehow I remembered those words like I did in the foster home's closet and a gush of peace ran over me. Strike two in the arena with Satan in the den of darkness, my biological mother's domain.

Another nine years later, Songbird was now sixteen and desired to visit her grandmother Lupe. How could I say no? I hoped perhaps, maybe, Lupe had been convicted of her past mistakes and would be a better example to her sixteen-year-old granddaughter. During those sixteen years, I still made it a point to visit her once or twice a year as I also did Mr. and Mrs. H. So it wasn't as if we were completely estranged. I have always had a tendency to continuously hope for the best in people, forgive repeatedly, and trust that God has my back. However, others have free choice and Lupe continued in her darkness. Unfortunately, a week with Grandma turned Songbird against me and she now had a new adoration for Grandma Lupe. Grandma Lupe was fun while I was strict.

Grandma took Songbird out for one more good time and told me I could meet them at Denny's in San Joaquin. This was the very same Denny's I had worked at when Songbird was abandoned. Why not Dos Palos? Why San Joaquin in Denny's? It wasn't until decades later that it occurred to me; perhaps the Lord wanted that scene to be relived. Perhaps

He wanted me to remember back to the point of reference when I had initially allowed Lupe to so negatively impact Songbird's and my life.

As I parked my car, I couldn't wait to hug my girl, love her, and take her home. As I looked through the windows I saw my mother and Songbird were sitting with a couple of strangers who were probably footing the bill. My baby girl Songbird wasn't anxious to see me; rather, she was giggly and intoxicated. Three strikes you're out. I had placed my daughter's life in the devil's den three times in a span of sixteen years. How could I give my innocent lamb to the devil? I had made the conscious decision to succumb to my sixteen year old daughter's pressure and to give my mother another chance but I never considered the possibility that I was handing my gift to Satan, a wolf dressed in an apron and smiles! Years later I still have deep regret for those times I allowed my daughter in the devil's den. Yet, I know I can't change the past, I can only trust my future to the One who has forgiven my past.

I don't know what I thought of my mother—I didn't consider her at the time, only my girl. It was a long drive home filling her up with coffee. Certainly I was not spending the night at my mother's and the long 5-hour ride home gave me time to think. Whose fault was this, Songbird's, my mother's, or mine? Surely if I had said, "No, you can't go," I would have risked Songbird running anyway. Surely the Lord allowed it?

Songbird was now acquainted with the party atmosphere, thank you, Lupe. She believed she was a little more successful as a cool teenager and was ready to try new things like lying, drinking, and partying behind my back. Others tell me this is typical teenage rebellion as they cut their umbilical cord, yet I felt her time with Lupe had been seriously detrimental.

I now worked at a men's prison as a guard and carried a .38 revolver and when in uniform I looked just like a cop. One night, I heard about a party Songbird wanted to attend in Los Osos, where we owned a home. I told Songbird she could not attend this party because there would be booze and maybe drugs. Songbird didn't come home from school on Friday and I instinctively knew where she was. I crashed this party in uniform. Teenagers were scrambling like cockroaches when I entered calling Songbird's name to get out and go home. She did and that was the end of her being invited to parties for a season.

At eighteen, Songbird graduated from high school. She became popular again after I rented a chauffeur and Rolls-Royce for her graduation party (oh, how fickle we are!) For her graduation gift, she wanted to visit her grandpa and uncles in San Diego. Since there had been no more troublesome incidents and she did graduate with A's, I agreed.

I never in a million years would have thought my brothers would shoot her up with heroin, then leave her at a Greyhound bus station alone where two men would shove her into the back of their van, take turns raping her, then throw her out of their moving van! A doctor happened to be in the vehicle behind the van when she was tossed. I got a call from a hospital rape counselor informing me of my daughter's situation. I wanted to drive and pick Songbird up, but the hospital staff said Songbird had insisted on going to the bus depot so she could get home. She didn't want me to pick her up.

Songbird refused to be seen by our hometown rape crisis support team when she arrived. I didn't understand that decision at the time. Later I discovered she was more fearful of the heroin inside her than the post-traumatic stress she was shoving down inside of herself. It was many years later before Songbird finally confided that her heroin addiction started with my brothers on her senior trip.

She refused counseling but started attending a beauty college. I thought Songbird was going to be okay. I thought life was going to get better. There was much prayer going on for my little family and me. I was well acquainted with the Vineyard Church in Los Osos, so I thought maybe we were all healed and off to a new start. Little did I realize that the bad habits and sins of my mother and brothers were instilled into Songbird, but the party animal was still alive and upon Songbird.

We moved to Long Beach. I had a great job at McDonnell Douglas, changed my name and occupation as the shelter for battered women helped us escape from Los Osos where my abusive husband lived. It was a fresh start, but Songbird and a girlfriend took one more ride. The innocent and smiling faces of two young men (wolves in sheep's clothing) picked them up for a ride to a party. They didn't drive them to a party: they drove the girls to Colorado and pimped them out. Two teenage girls just wanting to have fun but under the influence of the demon named 'good time.' Do you know anyone with this nickname, 'Good time?' Beware! Don't be blind to it like I was.

I didn't hear from Songbird or her girlfriend. Her brother didn't know where she went and their friends didn't have any contact from them. It was as if they had vanished! I prayed, cried, begged, sought out the law, thinking any day God would bring her home. I didn't have a cell phone in those days, just an office phone and hoped Songbird had my number. I starred at the phone hoping she would call me. I thought perhaps she ran away to get married and her best friend was with her or maybe vice versa. Songbird was a follower most of her life, as she was trained to obey and not ask questions. I should have been teaching her that she was the firstborn and therefore a natural born leader. But I was unacquainted with that concept until later in my adult life.

Every time my phone rang, I hoped it was her. I postponed lots of trips away from my phone so I would be available when she called. Ten days later, I got the call. "Mom, I need help, I can't talk or they will"... click. No voice. I was elated to know she was still alive, but scared and unsure... what next except to pray and let my fellowship know I had heard from her and she needed help. I felt helpless and frantic. I thought, "We need to pray harder, longer; what else can we do?" "Father, please help my unbelief, please bring my daughter home, please help her call, please let me be at the phone when she calls again!"

A few days later, she called again, "Mom, I am in Denver, Colorado, on a well-known prostitution street. I can't talk. We are here every night. Please, help me Mom, please. I love you. I am sorry, Mom, please help me!" I immediately got on the phone with churches in the Denver, Colorado, area and told them the situation. They were aware of that prostitution area. They asked me for her picture and anything else that could identify her. A group from the church roamed the streets that night until they found her. She was in a crowd but God's crowd was more powerful. The church group squeezed into the middle of the crowd, formed a circle around Songbird, let her know that her mother had called on them, kept her safe until they were able to usher her into a vehicle, and then put her on an airplane home.

I can't remember the details of those moments—they are vague in my mind. I can only recall God's people rescued her amidst darkness. The airlines, the churches, the date, the time, her girlfriend, everything except Songbird is a blur. All I was focused on was that my daughter was on her way home, alive! "Thank you, Jesus, for the physical rescue!"

She had been bruised but not broken, suffered but not perplexed. Through all this suffering, she had Jesus living in her heart and she never gave up. What was her secret in her valley of shadows of darkness? She accepted His resurrected spirit when she was a little girl and even though she turned her back on God, He never turned His back on her. Surely you can see there was a precious moment in this madness. Songbird considers her greatest gift the gift of 'long suffering.' The Bible calls it a fruit of the Spirit, *"But the fruit of the Spirit is love, joy, peace, longsuffering, kindness, goodness, faithfulness, gentleness, self-control...."* (Galatians 5:22–23 NKJV)

If we are God's kids, we can expect the world will treat us just like they treated Jesus. The world tried to kill His spirit and his mission too, but not even death could keep Him in the ground. He rose and so will His children. Stand firm! If you are being sought after by all the things the world has to offer, it may be a good indication you are about to walk into the devil's den. Jesus won't force you—He is a gentleman and will politely wait for you to make your choice. But He is there to rescue you and to lead you to a life more abundant if you are willing. Where do you want to spend eternity, in heaven or hell?

Both Songbird's and my stories are painful yet we believe; we believe, therefore we live. Why do we live filled with hope, love, faith, and peace? Because our Father and His Holy Spirit lives within us. He stands at every-one's door knocking to let Him come in! *"Behold, I stand at the door, and knock: if any man hear my voice, and open the door, I will come in to him, and will sup with him, and he with me.*" (Revelation 3:20 KJV)

My mother's murder was perhaps a little less dramatic, but none the less traumatic. Most of her life was a mess and I would never have expected she would end up in Heaven! But I am blessed to know she rests in Heaven now. I had heard the saying "It will be a cold day in hell" and I admit I actually thought "It would be a cold day in hell before my mother or father ever came to Jesus!"

I chose to keep my little family away from the influences of San Joaquin Valley and only visited once a year, usually around the Christmas season. I guess I wanted my children to know why we didn't have family like other families do, so once a year we would venture to the Valley and play Santa Claus.

My mother, Lupe, once told me she really didn't like it when I came around because she always felt she had to clean up the beer cans and bottles. Although I never said a word about the mess, she must have felt convicted and she resented me for it. There was always an underlying tension between us. Truthfully, it was just easier to stay away.

One day about five years before she was murdered, Lupe called to tell me she was going blind, a complication of her diabetes. She just wanted to call me at least once while she could still see the dials. I didn't know how to respond to that but it was hurtful to think, "Wow, it took blindness to consider calling me, really?" But God works in all things. *"And we know that in all things God works for the good of those who love him, who have been called according to his purpose.* (Romans 8:28 NIV) It was that call which prompted me to visit her alone, without either of our children present. I called her the next morning with a plan I knew she would love. I needed to get her undivided attention in order to have an important conversation.

She loved visiting a weight-loss doctor in Delhi. It cost her $25.00 for a diet shot and a week's worth of diet pills. I asked her if she would like to go with me and I would foot the bill. "Oh yes, when?"

I said, "Tomorrow morning." Yes, I had a job; but I took the day off. I felt this conversation was imperative. I knew God was directing me down this path. I picked her up and it dawned on me that this was the very first time my mother had been in my car. I loved it, she was my captive audience!

My mother was speechless the entire 3 hour drive as she listened to all the ways God had worked in my life. I began with the Catholic Church experience which she remembered quite well. It was the day we were taken from her. But my life long journey of one miracle after another, well she had never heard such stories. I wove our conversation into Biblical stories. For example, I shared the Lazarus story and told my mother he was dead and unable to pray for himself, therefore those around him were praying for him like I was praying for her. I shared the Bible verse where Jesus talked about "faith as small as a mustard seed" and I showed her the tiny mustard seed in a vial I carried in my car. She believed because she heard....It's in the hearing that they believe. *"So faith comes from hearing, and hearing through the word of Christ."* (Romans 10:17 ESV)

I talked about how Jesus healed the blind man. I said, "Mom, Jesus can drop the scales from your eyes if you just have this much faith," pointing to the vial. I continued, "As a matter if you let me pray with you, Jesus will see you have mustard seed size faith. He can make you whole again. Do you want me to pray with you?" I was hoping for a yes but really had no idea what she would say. I know God doesn't take me on a journey without giving me provisions and He doesn't open doors and then slam them in my face.

She said, "Yes, I want you to pray for me."

I said, "No, Mom, I will pray with you and for you." I pulled over on a dirt road and told her the story I tell everyone who hasn't accepted Jesus as their Savior. "Momma, Jesus is standing at your heart's door knocking, hoping you will answer the door and let Him in. However, I need you to consider this: when you're going on a date in your car or they are coming over to your house, you like to clean it, right?"

Of course, she said yes. "Well, the Lord needs us to ask Him to clean us out, forgive us for all our sins, cleanse us, but the very first question is, "Do you believe that Jesus is the Son of God, that He died on a cross and rose up from the dead, do you believe that?"

She said, "Yes."

"Well, Mom, do you want to ask Jesus to forgive you and come live inside of you?"

She said, "Yes."

I led her in the sinners' prayer of repentance. She asked Jesus to come live in her heart, her car, her home, and she was sorry for all her mistakes and sins. She was white as snow in the blink of an eye. A silly thought flashed through my mind, "This must be a cold day in hell." My son, Strongwind, led my dad to Jesus and I was privileged to lead my momma to Jesus! *"But now in Christ Jesus you who once were far away have been brought near by the blood of Christ."* (Ephesians 2:13 NIV)

As soon as she asked Jesus into her heart, I asked Jesus to please drop the scales from her eyes so she could see again. He did, immediately. Amazing what the faith of a mustard seed can accomplish! All those years of torment, delusion, anger, madness, drinking, carousing—gone in a flash of a moment at the appearance of His majesty! *"'Come now, let us settle the matter,' says the LORD. 'Though your sins are like scarlet, they shall be as white as snow....'"* (Isaiah 1:18 NIV)

Before she got out of my car, she asked me if I wanted to know why she acted like she didn't like me as I was growing up and into my adult years? Of course I wanted to know. She said, "Daughter, I should have been teaching you things about Jesus, and here you were teaching me by your example. I was always proud of you, but too ashamed to show you. I knew I hadn't been a good mother. I am sorry and I love you."

When my mother got home, she cleared her home of all paraphernalia and tuned her radio to Swaggart's Christian music, purposefully turning up the volume so the neighbors could hear. She joined a local church, cooked for the church, and volunteered for Seniors Meals on Wheels.

She started a new habit of reading her Bible. I shared some verses with her and she would search for them in her Bible. As she searched, she was washed with a brand-new spirit, heart, and mind. She said she wished she'd done the "Jesus thing" thirty years ago, because there hadn't been one lonely day since He came to live within her.

For the first time in her life she was reading the Bible and schooled me on verses she knew God was speaking directly to her: She was especially excited when she read that the Lord was building her a house and as soon as it was done, He was going to come and get her. She asked, "Did you know that?" I pretended NOT to know as I could see how joyful she was to teach me something about Jesus and His word. She loved that scripture and knew it was the truth. *"In My Father's house are many mansions; if it were not so, I would have told you. I go to prepare a place for you. And if I go and prepare a place for you, I will come again and receive you to Myself; that where I am, there you may be also."* (John 14:2-3 NKJV)

That day came sooner than we anticipated. On Saturday afternoons she was in the habit of picking up a friend who was confined to a wheelchair. He lived in Dos Palos and she would drive him to Atwater where she would gather fruits and vegetables and distribute them. He was a family friend who appreciated anyone picking him up and sharing their time with him. She was on her way to take him home after a long day but wanted to drop off her fruit first so it wouldn't spoil. Dos Palos was nearly 40 miles from her home. As she pulled into her long driveway, some of the neighbors tried to warn her about a man who was looking for her. They said he smelled of alcohol.

No sooner had my mother parked when a man walked out of her bushes. He shot her passenger first and then as she stood at her car door, he shot her in the head. Her passenger lived but my mother died instantly. Surely the Lord had finished her mansion and He came to get her. His will be done.

The **precious moment** in this hell was knowing my mother had accepted Jesus as her Savior. Her last days on earth were her most glorious and joyful and she now rests safely in His arms.

THE PURPOSE

"Now Jesus did many other signs in the presence of the disciples, which are not written in this book; but these are written so that you may believe that Jesus is the Christ, the Son of God, and that by believing you may have life in his name.

JOHN 20:30–31 ESV

"For You are my lamp, O Lord; The Lord shall enlighten my darkness."

2 SAMUEL 22:29 NKJV

L ike the apostle John, I haven't written all the miracles that Jesus has performed in my life, but these I have told because I believe the purpose for my survival from my hell on earth is to tell some of these wondrous, **precious moments** and share a few of His mighty miracles.

Satan has attacked me throughout my life, yet it was merely a table set before me in the presence of my enemies. Jesus defeated Satan on the cross. He took away the sting of death, bearing our sins and making a way for reconciliation between God and us; then He sent a Helper. *"And I will ask the Father, and he will give you another advocate to help you and be with you forever."* (John 14:16 NIV)

I love that I can cry out to my Helper and witness the miracles Jesus still performs today. He doesn't need me but I am so blessed when He uses me. Sometimes, just stepping out of my house, I am called to approach a stranger who didn't ask me anything or even acknowledge I exist, but I sense God nudging me to ask if I can pray for them. In all my life, I have only had one person refuse prayer. People, whether they know it or not, need God! I encourage you to be bold in your faith and ask others if you can pray for them. You will be amazed at how God can and will use you if you make yourself available.

There was one young girl named Amber who was always receptive to my prayers. I felt an instant connection with Amber and came to think of her as my adopted daughter. Amber's mom figuratively kicked her to the curb, when she was around twelve or thirteen years old. The mother could see no good in her daughter and constantly belittled her. Amber left home in order to run from her mom's madness. I, on the other hand, could only see the good nature of this young girl and continued to love her through her jail time, multiple births, and all her ups and downs. I fell in love with her as a mother loves a child; just as I am sure God falls in love with all His children; He is after all our Father!

One day Amber called and I could hear the desperation in her voice. She was feeling hopeless and alone. She was a single mom raising a son and so giving up wasn't an option; Amber reached out to me, knowing I loved her and also loved Jesus. My heart told me it was time to pay her a personal visit and pray for her. Simple as it sounds, I know it isn't always easy to pray, believing that the Holy Spirit hears us. But I can confidently attest to the fact that He does indeed; in fact He already knows our struggles before we utter the words. *"You have searched me, Lord, and you know me. You know when I sit and when I rise; you perceive my thoughts from afar. You discern my going out and my lying down; you are familiar with all my ways. Before a word is on my tongue you, Lord, know it completely."* (Psalm 139:1–4 NIV)

I held Amber's and her small son's hands and we prayed for her strength and for God's provision in her life. A few days later, completely out of the blue, a man who was living in North Carolina called Amber.

He had known her since high school. After high school, they had gone different ways but he had kept her picture in his wallet. He had never stopped loving her. As they talked, they reconnected and rekindled their relationship. She wanted to know my thoughts. Of course I believe God heard our prayers asking for His provision for this lonely young woman. His timing is always just right! I told her, "Only God can perform such a miracle, and He obviously opened the door for love—go through it!" They have been happily married for many years now and have built a beautiful life together. They both acknowledge their lives and love are a gift from God.

In 2009–2012, I decided I needed to further my education. I selected the college where one of my favorite pastors graduated from, California Baptist University. The pastor, Rick Warren of Saddle Back church, wrote a book called *Purpose Driven Life*. I had the opportunity to teach a Bible Study from that book in my home at 222, the miraculous home God gave me, but I digress.

After California Baptist University, I felt God prompting me to go back to truck driver. I thought to myself, "Well, that's a ridiculous thought." I had a conversation with God that went something like this: "After an upper division college, you want me to become a truck driver again? Why would you send me to Nineveh, Lord?" I resisted like Jonah, but the Lord shut doors to any occupation for which I was fully qualified. No one on the planet needed my skill set, not even a babysitting job! "Really? Funny God, real funny!" Jesus called us friends so I often speak to God as I would a friend.

I know God's hand when He is trying to position me; it isn't always comfortable but it's necessary. I've learned when you have God calling the shots, why fight it. He obviously has the upper hand. Admittedly, I don't always recognize his hand in the situation immediately. So, eighteen months later, I finally submitted to His leading and started seeking another truck driving position. The problem was that in the trucking industry if you haven't driven within the past six months, you must go back to square one and retrain. God handled that too! To make a long

191

story short, the McGrew family hired me to teach their S.W.A.T. team. S.W.A.T. stood for Southwest Area Transportation. Having this acronym on my resume was my ticket back into truck driving which is where God needed me to be at a specific point in time in order to heal my broken, addicted daughter and also to provide a dying man his final wish as God met him there. The Lord used the McGrew family to put me back on the road in His perfect timing. They were God sent, His helpers—angels in disguise.

During this time, my youngest daughter who was serving in the Air Force called to tell me she had cancer. With this particular cancer it was possible she might become barren. I immediately rebuked the doctor's diagnosis and knew Satan was coming to rob, steal, and destroy yet another part of me through my children. Satan is good at attacking our loved ones when he can't take us down. But rebuking Satan and sending him back to the pits of darkness has been a prayer where God intercedes for me quickly. And God didn't let us down! Two grandsons later, we are still singing praises!

In the Old Testament we read about Abraham and Sarah to whom, in their old age, God promised a son. He opened Sarah's womb and she conceived. Another womb that God opened was my son's best friend's wife. She wasn't able to conceive and they so wanted to have children. We were together at my son's fortieth birthday party when I asked her if she would allow me to pray for her on the sands of Bolsa Chica. Her son is now ten years old! Thank you, Father, for always hearing and answering my cries! *"Before they call I will answer; while they are still speaking I will hear."* (Isaiah 65:24 NIV)

Another opportunity presented itself, it was actually another door for me to walk through—literally. I temporarily moved out of the home I owned so my pregnant daughter and her husband could have a place to stay. I thought God intended to cross my path with someone who needed prayer or testimony so I was certain He had a specific place and purpose for me to move. He provided that accommodation in Melinda Lamb's home.

Melinda certainly is one of those angels in disguise. She has a big heart and opened her door to me. At this point in her life, it seemed she was giving and caring for everyone, including her very needy neighbor. It was draining! She definitely needed prayer for strength and guidance. I felt she deserved a loving, supportive mate so we prayed. I never know how God will respond to my prayers; yes, no, or wait, but I do know He loves to surprise us! I trust that He knows best, so I just pray and tell God, "Your will not mine be done"; then I let Him take over. By exercising our faith of a mustard seed, we prayed seeking God's best will; not surprisingly, great things happened!

One day shortly after we prayed, Melinda met a gentleman. He had actually built her home years before. Well, magically, or perhaps by God's design, they fell in love, had a Cinderella wedding, and became the Captain Morgan couple. They built and owned the Rosemarie a 55' house boat and turned it into the Captain Morgan's Delta Adventures on the California Delta, and blessed everyone who ever stood upon their vessel.

I previously mentioned that when God uses me, I am usually the one blessed. Such was the case in this story because later Captain and Mrs. Morgan gave me the honor of being their real estate agent. I sold her home, earning a commission which provided a full year's income. What a miracle! God is way ahead of us, knowing our needs in advance! He loves to surprise us with blessing upon blessing! The Morgans are still happily married. I must add this, they also have an island to sell in Northern California. I guess happily ever after can happen when God is in your corner! By the way, did I mention they have an island for sale in Northern California?

Another time God saw me through a difficult time and gave me a **precious moment in hell** was when I had to deal with the consequences of someone who had drug and alcohol addictions. A little dab will do you; that was a jingle from a Brylcreem commercial years ago. A little dab can actually be too much in the case of drugs and alcohol.

When someone first goes down the path of drugs or alcohol, it isn't normally their intent to become an addict or an alcoholic. That very first time turns into a next and then a next. Before long, they are searching for their next 'dab' which eventually causes them to rob, steal, and destroy anything in their way of getting that fix. They will take whatever is available in their immediate vicinity and will reach into any pocket book: mother, father, brothers, sisters, friends; they don't care.

One year, two of my children treated me to a couple of vacations! It was my first time out of the country. Strongwind took me on a cruise to Mexico; then Ebb-oni, grandsons, and I went to Europe. I was elated to be enjoying vacations with my children and grandchildren!

When I got back home, it was time to pay my bills. However, while I was gone someone depleted my bank account. No matter how much discussion I had with the bank, they couldn't help me. I would have to wait until my next Social Security check, which meant I couldn't pay my rent. I was forced to move. I couldn't bring myself to impose on Ebb-oni or Strongwind, so I had to put my belongings in storage and wait out the storm until I could gather enough money to rent again. It was a low blow.

It took nearly six months to finally get a shelter again. Not only was I out on the street, but Songbird lived with me, so both of us were homeless. I know God doesn't abandon us and for some unknown reason, my Comforter allowed this event to unfold; perhaps He wanted me to experience just a bit of what other homeless folks face.

It wasn't quite as bad as it could have been. I at least owned a car outright, so no one could repossess it. But how would we put gas in it, where would we park, where would we go to the bathroom, what would we eat? If we didn't have gas we couldn't even drive to a homeless shelter! There wasn't a day that went by that I didn't cry. I wasn't accustomed to being homeless, but Songbird knew the lifestyle—she had been there before. This actually turned out to be helpful to me because I just didn't know the ropes! Songbird could make a dollar become a meal at McDonalds: asking for a dollar meal and having extras put on it like tomatoes and lettuce was ingenious. However, it was challenging finding a place to park and sleeping in the car with a 150 pound dog was a tight squeeze. It was worth the discomfort though as Biggy, Songbird's service dog, was a great deterrent to unwanted attention and warned off anyone who got too close.

By the grace of God, Songbird and I survived and there were some **precious moments** in this too. While we stayed in free campsites, we were showered with stars and enjoyed God's great outdoors. For the first time we had an opportunity to spend mother-daughter time together, something we were unable to do when Songbird was young. In those earlier years I was too busy with work, school, and the craziness of being a single mom. There simply had not been time for that one-on-one relationship. Perhaps it was an odd circumstance for a blessing, but God allowed this situation and with it He provided a unique opportunity for us to rectify the earlier loss of our mother-daughter time. That time was the beginning of her restored life. We started at ground zero and she rose to the top of a mountain in the perfect California city, SLO, where she serves Jesus and enjoys her new life.

Over the years there were several times when family members, addicted to drugs, stole, robbed, and attempted to destroy my life, yet God brought me through it all. And what's more, because God has forgiven me much and His Holy Spirit lives in me, I am able to forgive others as well. The ability to forgive is God's gift to us. It allowed me to be a witness and through God's mercy and grace each broken, addicted family member turned to serve a risen Savior instead of serving their drugs. Surely just a little dab of Jesus turns the course of one's destiny.

God is the Alpha and Omega, the Beginning and the End; of course He can preplan and reposition us so that certain people cross our paths at just the right time. Our God is a God of order as well as a God of Solutions! The woman helping me edit this book is one God maneuvered into my life and then laid it on her heart to assist me. She is very active, travels the world, has a large family so lots of company, and volunteers in various ways; she is constantly on the go. But just at the moment I needed help with organizing my book and then again when the book was ready for the final editing, God cleared her calendar for several weeks at a time! God knew this book would still be a rough draft and not ready for print if it wasn't for His intervention!

There are so many more stories—but again the apostle John comes to mind. *"Jesus did many other things as well. If every one of them were written down, I suppose that even the whole world would not have room for the books that would be written."* (John 21:25 NIV)

The stories I have shared are meant to testify to how He will always be there to see you through the valleys of darkness. If you have read this book, I believe God has a purpose in that. The Word says, *"For we are God's handiwork, created in Christ Jesus to do good works, which God prepared in advance for us to do."* (Ephesians 2:10 NIV) Did He send me into your shadow of darkness as a witness to you? I hope so! Jesus changed my life. He has walked with me through my shadows of darkness and He rescued me. He has given me a purpose. He can do that for you as well. Proverbs 19:20-21 (NIV) says, *"Listen to advice and accept discipline, and at the end you will be counted among the wise. Many are the plans in a person's heart, but it is the Lord's purpose that prevails."*

Father in Jesus name, only You know the plans You have for us when You create us and place us in our mothers' wombs. Your Word says, You are the potter and we are the clay. Father many are lost and without hope yet YOU are all-knowing and have plans for each person in whose hands You have placed this book. Please Father, I ask that You fill each reader with Your Almighty Holy Spirit and allow them to be lifted and encouraged right where they are. I plead Your almighty, everlasting, blood upon their lives and circumstances. May Your will prevail even when they can't hear, feel, or see Your hand at work. Let them know YOU are in control and may Your light shine upon them in this dark world. Thank you Father for never leaving us or forsaking us. Your will Father, not mine, be done. Amen.

BIBLE REFERENCE

INTRODUCTION

Romans 8:28
(English Standard Version)

And we know that for those who love God all things work together for good, for those who are called according to his purpose.

2 Timothy 3:10-11
(English Standard Version)

You, however, have followed my teaching, my conduct, my aim in life, my faith, my patience, my love, my steadfastness, my persecutions and sufferings that happened to me at Antioch, at Iconium, and at Lystra—which persecutions I endured; yet from them all the Lord rescued me.

CHAPTER 1

Psalm 23:4
(King James Version)

Yea, though I walk through the valley of the shadow of death, I will fear no evil: for thou art with me

CHAPTER 2

Psalm 10:14
(New International Version)

But you, God, see the trouble of the afflicted; you consider their grief and take it in hand. The victims commit themselves to you; you are the helper of the fatherless.

2 Corinthians 11:14-15
(New American Standard Bible)

No wonder, for even Satan disguises himself as an angel of light. Therefore it is not surprising if his servants also disguise themselves as servants of righteousness, whose end will be according to their deeds.

John 11:35
(English Standard Version)

"Jesus wept."

Revelation 7:17
(New King James Version)

for the Lamb who is in the midst of the throne will shepherd them and lead them to living fountains of waters. And God will wipe away every tear from their eyes.

Psalm 56:8
(New American Standard Bible)

You have taken account of my wanderings; Put my tears in Your bottle; Are they not in Your book?

Hebrews 10:22
(New American Standard Bible)

let us draw near with a sincere heart in full assurance of faith, having our hearts sprinkled clean from an evil conscience and our bodies washed with pure water.

1 Corinthians 6:11
(English Standard Version)

And such were some of you. But you were washed, you were sanctified, you were justified in the name of the Lord Jesus Christ and by the Spirit of our God.

2 Corinthians 5:17
(New King James Version)

Therefore, if anyone is in Christ, he is a new creation; old things have passed away; behold, all things have become new.

CHAPTER 3

Psalm 34:18
(New International Version)

The Lord is close to the brokenhearted and saves those who are crushed in spirit.

Isaiah 40:29
(New International Version)

He gives strength to the weary and increases the power of the weak.

CHAPTER 4

Psalm 19:1
(New International Version)

The heavens declare the glory of God; the skies proclaim the work of His hands.

Job 37:5
(New Living Translation)

God's voice is glorious in the thunder. We can't even imagine the greatness of his power.

CHAPTER 5

Proverbs 3:12
(Good News Translation)

The LORD corrects those he loves, as parents correct a child of whom they are proud.

Luke 23:34
(New International Version)

Jesus said, "Father, forgive them, for they do not know what they are doing." And they divided up his clothes by casting lots.

James 1:5
(English Standard Version)

If any of you lacks wisdom, let him ask God, who gives generously to all without reproach, and it will be given him.

Ephesians 4:32
(English Standard Version)

Be kind to one another, tenderhearted, forgiving one another, as God in Christ forgave you.

John 10:10
(English Standard Version)

The thief comes only to steal and kill and destroy. I came that they may have life and have it abundantly.

Matthew 4:8-9
(English Standard Version)

Again, the devil took him to a very high mountain and showed him all the kingdoms of the world and their glory. And he said to him, "All these I will give you, if you will fall down and worship me."

Matthew 4:10
(English Standard Version)

Then Jesus said to him, "Be gone, Satan! For it is written, You shall worship the Lord your God and him only shall you serve."

CHAPTER 6

2 Corinthians 6:14
(English Standard Version)

Do not be unequally yoked with unbelievers. For what partnership has righteousness with lawlessness? Or what fellowship has light with darkness?

Luke 1:37
(New King James Version)

For with God nothing will be impossible.

CHAPTER 7

Hebrews 8:12
(New King James Version)

For I will be merciful to their unrighteousness, and their sin and their lawless deeds I will remember no more.

Psalm 37:4
(New International Version)

Delight yourself in the LORD, and He will give you the desires of your heart.

Psalm 37:23
(New Living Translation)

The Lord directs the steps of the Godly. He delights in every detail of their lives.

Matthew 7:1
(King James Version)

Judge not, that ye be not judged.

1 John 1:9
(King James Version)

If we confess our sins, He is faithful and just to forgive us our sins and to cleanse us from all unrighteousness.

Romans 3:22-24
(New International Version)

This righteousness is given through faith in Jesus Christ to all who believe. There is no difference between Jew and Gentile, for all have sinned and fall short of the glory of God, and all are justified freely by his grace through the redemption that came by Christ Jesus.

John 3:16
(King James Version)

For God so loved the world, that he gave his only begotten Son, that whosoever believeth in him should not perish, but have everlasting life.

CHAPTER 8

James 1:17
(New International Version)

Every good and perfect gift is from above, coming down from the Father of the heavenly lights, who does not change like shifting shadows.

1 John 4:4
(New King James Version)

You are of God, little children, and have overcome them, because He who is in you is greater than he who is in the world.

CHAPTER 9

Numbers 12:6
(New King James Version)

Then He said, "Hear now My words: If there is a prophet among you, I, the LORD, make Myself known to him in a vision; I speak to him in a dream."

CHAPTER 10

Proverbs 3:6
(New International Version)

in all your ways submit to him, and he will make your paths straight.

1 Corinthians 10:23
(New International Version)

"I have the right to do anything," you say—but not everything is beneficial. "I have the right to do anything"—but not everything is constructive.

Matthew 12:31
(New International Version)

And so I tell you, every kind of sin and slander can be forgiven, but blasphemy against the Spirit will not be forgiven.

Psalm 23:6
(New King James Version)

Surely goodness and mercy shall follow me all the days of my life: and I will dwell in the house of the LORD for ever.

John 15:13
(New International Version)

Greater love has no one than this: to lay down one's life for one's friends.

2 Corinthians 12:2
(English Standard Version)

I know a man in Christ who fourteen years ago was caught up to the third heaven—whether in the body or out of the body I do not know, God knows.

Proverbs 3:11-12
(New International Version)

My son, do not despise the LORD's discipline, and do not resent his rebuke, because the LORD disciplines those he loves, as a father the son he delights in.

CHAPTER 11

Mark 4:23
(New International Version)

If anyone has ears to hear, let them hear.

Ephesians 6:16
(New King James Version)

above all, taking the shield of faith with which you will be able to quench all the fiery darts of the wicked one.

Romans 12:20
(New International Version)

On the contrary: "If your enemy is hungry, feed him; if he is thirsty, give him something to drink. In doing this, you will heap burning coals on his head."

Matthew 5:44
(English Standard Version)

But I say to you, Love your enemies and pray for those who persecute you,

Romans 12:17
(New International Version)

Do not repay anyone evil for evil. Be careful to do what is right in the eyes of everyone.

CHAPTER 12

Matthew 5:11
(New King James Version)

Blessed are you when they revile and persecute you, and say all kinds of evil against you falsely for My sake.

Romans 12:18-19
(New International Version)

If it is possible, as far as it depends on you, live at peace with everyone. Do not take revenge, my dear friends, but leave room for God's wrath, for it is written: "It is mine to avenge; I will repay," says the Lord.

1 Peter 5:8
(English Standard Version)

Be sober-minded; be watchful. Your adversary the devil prowls around like a roaring lion, seeking someone to devour.

2 Timothy 1:7
(New King James Version)

For God has not given us a spirit of fear, but of power and of love and of a sound mind.

Jeremiah 33:3
(New King James Version)

Call to Me, and I will answer you, and show you great and mighty things, which you do not know.

Romans 8:31
(New International Version)

What, then, shall we say in response to these things? If God is for us, who can be against us?

CHAPTER 13

Proverbs 23:7
(New King James Version)

For as he thinks in his heart, so is he. "Eat and drink!" he says to you, But his heart is not with you.

Deuteronomy 31:8
(New International Version)

The LORD himself goes before you and will be with you; he will never leave you nor forsake you. Do not be afraid; do not be discouraged.

Deuteronomy 33:27
(New International Version)

The eternal God is your refuge, and underneath are the everlasting arms. He will drive out your enemies before you, saying, "Destroy them!"

John 16:33
(New International Version)

I have told you these things, so that in me you may have peace. In this world you will have trouble. But take heart! I have overcome the world.

Romans 8:18
(New Living Translation)

Yet what we suffer now is nothing compared to the glory he will reveal to us later.

Revelation 21:4
(New King James Version)

And God will wipe away every tear from their eyes; there shall be no more death, nor sorrow, nor crying. There shall be no more pain, for the former things have passed away.

**Ecclesiastes 4:9-10
(English Standard Version)**

Two are better than one, because they have a good reward for their toil. For if they fall, one will lift up his fellow. But woe to him who is alone when he falls and has not another to lift him up!

**Joshua 24:15
(New King James Version)**

And if it seems evil to you to serve the Lord, choose for yourselves this day whom you will serve, whether the gods which your fathers served that were on the other side of the River, or the gods of the Amorites, in whose land you dwell. But as for me and my house, we will serve the Lord.

**2 Peter 3:8
(English Standard Version)**

But do not overlook this one fact, beloved, that with the Lord one day is as a thousand years, and a thousand years as one day.

CHAPTER 14

**John 20:30-31
(New International Version)**

Jesus performed many other signs in the presence of his disciples, which are not recorded in this book. But these are written that you may believe that Jesus is the Messiah, the Son of God, and that by believing you may have life in his name.

**Matthew 18:20
(King James Version)**

For where two or three are gathered together in my name, there am I in the midst of them.

CHAPTER 15

**Mark 9:23-24
(New International Version)**

"If you can?" said Jesus. "Everything is possible for one who believes." Immediately the boy's father exclaimed, "I do believe; help me overcome my unbelief!"

**John 20:25
(New International Version)**

So the other disciples told him, "We have seen the Lord!" But he said to them, "Unless I see the nail marks in his hands and put my finger where the nails were, and put my hand into his side, I will not believe."

John 20:27-28
(New International Version)

Then he said to Thomas, "Put your finger here; see my hands. Reach out your hand and put it into my side. Stop doubting and believe.' Thomas said to him, 'My Lord and my God!"

Romans 8:35, 38-39
(New International Version)

Who shall separate us from the love of Christ? Shall trouble or hardship or persecution or famine or nakedness or danger or sword? For I am convinced that neither death nor life, neither angels nor demons, neither the present nor the future, nor any powers, neither height nor depth, nor anything else in all creation, will be able to separate us from the love of God that is in Christ Jesus our Lord.

1 Corinthians 15:33
(New International Version)

Do not be misled: "Bad company corrupts good character."

Job 7:6
(English Standard Version)

My days are swifter than a weaver's shuttle and come to their end without hope.

Psalm 116:2
(New Living Translation)

Because he bends down to listen, I will pray as long as I have breath!

Proverbs 17:22
(New International Version)

A cheerful heart is good medicine, but a crushed spirit dries up the bones.

CHAPTER 16

Luke 9:62
(New American Standard Bible)

But Jesus said to him, "No one, after putting his hand to the plow and looking back, is fit for the kingdom of God."

CHAPTER 17

Esther 4:14
(New King James Version)

For if you remain completely silent at this time, relief and deliverance will arise for the Jews from another place, but you and your father's house will perish. Yet who knows whether you have come to the kingdom for such a time as this?

Isaiah 14:27
(New International Version)

For the LORD Almighty has purposed, and who can thwart him? His hand is stretched out, and who can turn it back?

CHAPTER 18

Ephesians 6:11
(New International Version)

Put on the full armor of God, so that you can take your stand against the devil's schemes.

Matthew 17:20
(English Standard Version)

He said to them, "Because of your little faith." For truly, I say to you, "if you have faith like a grain of mustard seed, you will say to this mountain, Move from here to there, and it will move, and nothing will be impossible for you."

Micah 5:12
(New International Version)

I will destroy your witchcraft and you will no longer cast spells.

Ephesians 6:11
(New International Version)

Put on the full armor of God, so that you can take your stand against the devil's schemes.

Numbers 26:10
(King James Version)

And the earth opened her mouth, and swallowed them up together with Korah, when that company died, what time the fire devoured two hundred and fifty men: and they became a sign.

CHAPTER 19

Acts 2:17
(English Standard Version)

And in the last days it shall be, God declares, that I will pour out my Spirit on all flesh, and your sons and your daughters shall prophesy, and your young men shall see visions, and your old men shall dream dreams;

Romans 12:6
(New International Version)

We have different gifts, according to the grace given to each of us. If your gift is prophesying, then prophesy in accordance with your faith;

Galatians 1:20
(New American Standard Bible)

Now in what I am writing to you, I assure you before God that I am not lying.

Mark 2:11
(New Life Version)

I say to you, "Get up. Take your bed and go to your home."

Ephesians 3:20
(New International Version)

Now to him who is able to do immeasurably more than all we ask or imagine, according to his power that is at work within us,

CHAPTER 20

Matthew 10:28
(New King James Version)

And do not fear those who kill the body but cannot kill the soul. But rather fear Him who is able to destroy both soul and body in hell.

Genesis 2:16-17
(New King James Version)

And the LORD God commanded the man, saying, "Of every tree of the garden you may freely eat; but of the tree of the knowledge of good and evil you shall not eat, for in the day that you eat of it you shall surely die."

Genesis 3:1
(New International Version)

Now the serpent was more crafty than any of the wild animals the LORD God had made. He said to the woman, "Did God really say, You must not eat from any tree in the garden?"

Genesis 3:4
(New International Version)

"You will not certainly die," the serpent said to the woman."

Genesis 3:6
(New International Version)

When the woman saw that the fruit of the tree was good for food and pleasing to the eye, and also desirable for gaining wisdom, she took some and ate it. She also gave some to her husband, who was with her, and he ate it.

Romans 3:23
(New International Version)

for all have sinned and fall short of the glory of God,

Romans 6:23
(New International Version)

For the wages of sin is death, but the gift of God is eternal life in Christ Jesus our Lord

Romans 5:8
(New International Version)

But God demonstrates his own love for us in this: While we were still sinners, Christ died for us.

Galatians 5:22-23
(New King James Version)

But the fruit of the Spirit is love, joy, peace, longsuffering, kindness, goodness, faithfulness, gentleness, self-control. Against such there is no law.

Revelation 3:20
(King James Version)

Behold, I stand at the door, and knock: if any man hear my voice, and open the door, I will come in to him, and will sup with him, and he with me.

Romans 10:17
(English Standard Version)

So faith comes from hearing, and hearing through the word of Christ.

Ephesians 2:13
(New International Version)

But now in Christ Jesus you who once were far away have been brought near by the blood of Christ.

Isaiah 1:18
(New International Version)

"Come now, let us settle the matter," says the LORD. *"Though your sins are like scarlet, they shall be as white as snow; though they are red as crimson, they shall be like wool."*

John 14:2-3
(New King James Version)

In My Father's house are mansions; if it were not so, I would have told you. I go to prepare a place for you. And if I go and prepare a place for you, I will come again and receive you to Myself; that where I am, there you may be also.

CHAPTER 21

John 20:30-31
(English Standard Version)

Now Jesus did many other signs in the presence of the disciples, which are not written in this book; but these are written so that you may believe that Jesus is the Christ, the Son of God, and that by believing you may have life in his name.

2 Samuel 22:29
(New King James Version)

For You are my lamp, O LORD; The LORD shall enlighten my darkness.

John 14:16
(New International Version)

And I will ask the Father, and he will give you another advocate to help you and be with you forever—

Psalm 139:1-4
(New International Version)

You have searched me, LORD, and you know me. You know when I sit and when I rise; you perceive my thoughts from afar. You discern my going out and my lying down; you are familiar with all my ways. Before a word is on my tongue you, LORD, know it completely.

Isaiah 65:24
(New International Version)

Before they call I will answer; while they are still speaking I will hear.

John 21:25
(New International Version)

Jesus did many other things as well. If every one of them were written down, I suppose that even the whole world would not have room for the books that would be written.

Ephesians 2:10
(New International Version)

For we are God's handiwork, created in Christ Jesus to do good works, which God prepared in advance for us to do.

LETTERS TO THE AUTHOR

Dear Charli, it's been 6 years and …I'm exhausted. I've felt alone, so alone and can't seem to get out of it. I lost my Mom, Uncle, Cousin, Sister, Brother, Jobs, and an amazing man. It's been hell and I've been steadfast in the hurt and pain of what has happened with each of those things. I've been on this journey for a long time now. After 8 years in the military and 3 tours under my belt in Iraq and Afghanistan; it's been traumatic to say the least. Seems sometimes like some sort of Groundhog Day. The days continue on and on. I've even contemplated suicide at my lowest of time.

These last few months I've had you on my mind. Funny enough, one day after work, I had seen your business card on my door the other day. How did you even know where I lived? Only God could have led you to my door. I asked myself, "Why is Charli here? What is this all about?" I contacted you a couple days later. Come to find out your writing a book about "Precious Moments in Hell". When I told you my story of the past six years you said, "Baby girl, you need to write about your years of hell and let the world know how you survive it, day by day. This will be your precious moment of liberation and you can tell the world about your military opposition and cry for Veteran's help."

Here we are! One week later and I sense a time for healing and restoration. In the past I haven't been able to say what I needed. I haven't had closure and I've envisioned a moment that would allow the truth to come out. I am broken and God knows it. I feel now, more than ever, that my mom would want her story told and who better to tell it then me. It's weighed heavily on my heart and mind for a long time.

2 years after getting out of the military I moved to North Carolina. I was turning 28, had a job and was going to college to complete my B.A. degree. I was also dealing with the death of one of my comrades and some PTSD issues. I hadn't seen Mom in three years. It was definitely time for us to see each other. The last time I had seen her was when my comrade, SPC M.S., died in 2011. We decided I would come to visit her in California for my birthday, Aug 28th, 2014. She had bought me a plane ticket and we were both elated for the time when we would get to see each other. There was so much catching up that needed to be done. I could tell by previous phone calls that she was getting worse. She was diagnosed with Huntingtons disease at 47 and she was now 56. She needed help. A lot of help. So much, that I should have been home with her and not in North Carolina. I shouldn't have trusted my brother and sister to take care of my mom the way I knew I could. My brother and sister were near her but not helping her the way she needed.

Let me give you a little background of my brother and sister. My brother Jake has always been a lot like our dad; selfish, a smoker, and the gamer type, who only cared about money and himself. Ever since I can remember he has been cold. I haven't seen him in almost 20 years. He's always been caulis and hard. Last time I talked with him was at mom's funeral. I asked for a relationship with him because I missed him and he said, "We just don't have anything in common".

My sister Winner was a run-away child. She was and its lifestyle and always in opposition to our mother. She started changing her life around in her mid-30's. I remember boyfriends popping in and out, her fighting with my mom and seeing her at detention centers. I remember her sending me letters saying that she missed me so much and that things would be different. We never really had a relationship; even when I offered to help her in her most recent pregnancy. We tried but she has always done something to mess things up with us.

So, after years of let downs between them both; it wasn't unusual that my brother and sister never let me know that my Mom was extremely sick.

Two weeks earlier my Mom and I had talked. It was the last conversation we had. She had called crying. I can remember her cry. She let me know that Jake suddenly left to move to Las Vegas and she needed help. I remember she needed to be seen regarding some stomach issues. At one point I even had to call up a friend to go and check on her and bring her diapers. That's how bad it was! From across country I started looking for agencies that could help her. I was frantic to find something. I was upset with my brother and sister for not being there to take better care of her, but there was nothing I could do. I had a job and I was completing my B.A. degree. Looking for help was the best I could do, not knowing she was deathly sick.

A few days prior to my trip home to see Mom, I realized I hadn't heard from her in a few days. This was unusual because we talked almost every day. This particular week she seemed distant but that was becoming normal due to her sickness.

Finally! It was my birthday. I landed in L.A. and shuttled to Moms. I remember everything in slow motion. Seems just like yesterday. It was a warm day. I smelled the fresh air and walked from the street where the taxi dropped me to my Moms porch. There was mail and a letter on the outside of her door. I took everything off of the door and set it aside and opened the screen. I opened the door and it was freezing. It smelled. Kind of like old food. I said, "Mom I'm home". I heard nothing. I moved from the living room to the kitchen to her room and then…I had seen the bathroom door open just a crack. I pushed it. All of a sudden, I had seen Mom's blue morphed puffy face with her bebe eyes staring right at me. A vision I'll never forget. I didn't know what I had just really seen. I couldn't believe it. I couldn't find a thought or process what was going on. Did I just see this? What do I do? I wanted to take her body and hug her. I wanted to hold her. But, I couldn't. She had been there for a nearly eight days. The blood on the sink and floor was dry and coagulated. I ran out the door and screamed. I didn't know what to do. I went to the neighbor's house and let them know. They took care of the rest. I was in shock the whole time. Within days of finding mom dead; my brother, sister and I went to her house to pack up her things. When I came to her house to see what was going on I couldn't even process.

Mom was gone now and I blamed it on my brother and sister. They did this to her! They never let me know that mom had been this bad. Jake left her to go to Vegas when he knew she was in horrible shape and Winner was tending to her "Family". OH! And how much of a nuisance my mom was. I get it. We have responsibilities, but we also have one mother.

Still in shock I remembered I had to go on my flight back home. I didn't have a ride back to the airport airport. Me and my Mom were supposed to spend the weekend together. Only, I got a short time to help prepare her funeral. I asked my sister and my brother for a ride, but they said they couldn't take me for whatever reason. I was extremely upset with Winner. I didn't understand why she couldn't help her sister with a ride. How insensitive of a person could she be. I yelled at her and let her know that she was being a jerk. Then, all of a sudden, I remember her fist coming towards me. She hit me! On my mom's property in front of my brother, brother in law, and nephew. I thought to myself in that moment, THAT'S IT! Winner and Jake where dead to me right then and there. I never thought 2 people could be so hateful towards me. FOR WHAT!? Because I cared? I don't remember how I got to my flight. It's still just a haze.

I can't recall all the details, but I can still see my Moms sad fixed eyes. I can still feel the loss. Now not only have I had to deal with the loss of my friend, the murder of my NCO, and the images of coffins of soldiers that didn't make it home being driven to C130s in Afghanistan; I had to deal with seeing my dead mother.

My sister never apologized to me for what she had done. Winner and Jake took complete control of all the final funeral arrangements. I never received ANY of my mom's belongings and didn't speak at the funeral because I was just so full of grief. I had been physically and mentally assaulted from my brother and sister and just had to take the blows.

I've died a little more each day, every day, since the day I has seen mom the way she was. I've lived every day with the WHAT IF's! God help me! I need help. Charli said, "Only God has the authority to create and take life and He always knows when He's finished building our home in Heaven. Then He comes and gets us". Yes, Mom could have had a more graceful and caring ending but that was ultimately up to my brother and sister.

3 Months after my mom's passing, I packed up my things from North Carolina and moved back to California. I didn't know what I was going to do. I just had a feeling in my heart to go. I felt for some reason that it would bring me closer to Mom.

Looking back at all the trials I've been through since then, I know it was all for a reason and God has helped to direct me.

He was there when I accidently almost burnt down my friend's house and got kicked out.

He was there when I got fired at a job with a Real Estate agent.

He was there when He sent Dee to have me stay with her in the mobile home.

He was there when He put it in my mind to move in the back house of where my mom lived. I felt that it was somehow being close to her and that I had a little piece of her next to me. Even with the trauma from seeing her dead.

He was there when I quit VETS.

He was there when I quit the dealership.

He was there when I got fired from Boys and Girls Clubs.

He was there through me finding and losing a new love.

He was there through me having a tumor and having to go through surgery.

He was there through my suicidal thoughts.

He was there through the lawyer and cousin battle.

He was there!

But it was all for a reason. If it wasn't for me moving home, I wouldn't be where I am today to tell my story. Things didn't work out in those situations because this truth needed to be told. I believe this with all my heart and hope that I can break free from the chains of so much grief in my heart. I am now the CEO of my own business and look forward to what God has in store. This story is the beginning of something amazing. I just know it. It's truly been my "Precious Moment in Hell".

My mom will not be forgotten. Her flame still burns. She is one who lead by example and she fought all her life for her family the best she knew how. She was strong, loved God, loved being an entrepreneur, loved riding horses, loved learning, loved food, and most of all loved her family and friends. Mom was truly my rock and I have her fighting spirit. She was always there when I needed her. She was there when I was in dance to encourage me, she was there at auditions rooting me on, she was there when I ran away from my dad's to live with her, She was there to throw a celebration for whatever it was that I was doing, She was there to listen to my good and bad times, she was there to sing with, she was there to laugh with, she was there when I was trying out for flag, she was there when I practice with my friends to try out for cheer, she was there when I graduated, she was there when I went to the military, she was there when I came home on my R&R from my deployments. she was there through the deaths of beloved friends; she was there most every step. And I feel like I wasn't there. I wasn't there to take care of her.

My brother and sister would tell you different of what their reality is. they would tell you differently of what they did and whose fault it was. They live a life now, that in some ways looks like they're just fine. They moved together back to North Carolina and are living their best lives from the money they received after my moms death. I whole heartedly believe they are responsible for my moms death. They will always be who they are and that will never change.

As these 6 years have passed and this moment came; I ask myself, "can I forgive them?" I don't know. I do know I believe in God. He had to be keeping me standing because I don't know how I've been doing this thing called life. Charli says, "The Holy Spirit lives in me. Therefore, I rise up again. Just like Jesus rose up from His deathly experience." This might be the hardest thing I've ever done. Because this isn't just my precious moment; this is my Mom's. I'm not speaking. Mom speaks through me. She has given me the courage to do what I needed for closure for both her and I. And now, we both get the chance, to stand up, and fight.

-Little Lu
(This letter is authorized to be published in Precious Moments in Hell)

CPSIA information can be obtained
at www.ICGtesting.com
Printed in the USA
LVHW080547130820
662904LV00003B/13